THEORY AND PRACTICE OF EDUCATION

Also available from Continuum

Theory of Education, David Turner
Philosophy of Education, Richard Pring
Education and Community, Dianne Gereluk
Private Education, Geoffrey Walford
Key Ideas in Educational Research, David Scott and Marlene Morrison

THEORY AND PRACTICE OF EDUCATION

DAVID A. TURNER

continuum

KH

Continuum International Publishing Group
The Tower Building, 11 York Road, London SE1 7NX
80 Maiden Lane, Suite 704, New York, NY 10038

www.continuumbooks.com

British Library Cataloguing-in-Publication Data
A catalogue record for this book is available from the British Library.

ISBN: 0-8264-9107-3 (hardback)

Library of Congress Cataloging-in-Publication Data
A catalog record for this book is available from the Library of Congress.

Typeset by Aarontype Limited, Easton, Bristol
Printed and bound in Great Britain by The Cromwell Press, Trowbridge, Wiltshire

8/25/08

Contents

List of figures

Chapter 1

Introduction

I have remarked elsewhere that the failure of policy-makers to engage with theory and the failure of researchers to provide a sound basis for policy-making is a relationship (or lack of relationship) that has fault on both sides (Turner 2004a). However, the greater fault undoubtedly lies with the researchers who have failed to provide models of sufficient complexity that they can be used effectively in the policy-making process.

It should be noted that in this context complexity is not a matter of how many variables are involved in the explanatory models, nor of how many factors are involved in a particular situation. Still less does it rest in the view that the human sciences cannot benefit from the experience of the physical sciences because human situations are inherently more complex than situations involving mere inanimate objects.

Complexity in the field of education studies, resides with the fact that everybody is involved in constructing their own education. Each of us is piecing together our own personality from the examples and cultural heritage with which we are presented. Everybody is creating their own life-story from their own experiences. At the core of each person is an active creator whose primary task is the construction of their own self. A life cannot be reduced to the constellation of 'factors' which gives it shape or structure. The complexity of education resides with the fact that it involves human beings, and that, perhaps more than in any other field, motivation, willpower, choice and interpersonal chemistry are crucial to the endeavour and do more to shape the outcome than background or prior experience.

At its most basic, when confronted with a challenging situation a human being can do one of two things: embrace the challenge, restructure their own understanding, accommodate to the new experience and change and hopefully grow as a result; or reject the challenge, refuse to reform their own knowledge and remain steadfast to principles that have been acquired earlier. This process is so firmly at the core of human learning and experience that it is difficult to describe it in neutral terms. As educationists we are so involved in confronting people with fresh experiences and expecting them to change, to incorporate that new learning into their way of thinking, that we are inclined to describe learning in positive terms and failure to learn in negative terms. However, that is much too simple. There are times when new experiences must be put aside and rejected. If Nelson Mandela had learned from his experience in prison that the inhuman apartheid regime was immovable, a whole range of positive consequences would have been lost. If everybody who was bullied learned from their experience that bullying was a good way to achieve one's ends, then educational institutions, and others, would be intolerable.

Rejecting the lessons of new experience, remaining steadfast to convictions and cultivating a scepticism of new information can all be as commendable as learning. Indeed, learning too quickly, achieving the superficial understanding of the newly converted, is almost never desirable. So, in taking a stance of acceptance or resistance in the face of new experience, one cannot assume that the moral balance is always weighted in favour of the former.

Of course, we all know that too ready a recourse to resistance is all too likely to close one off from new experiences and prematurely curtail learning. 'I can't do sums', or, 'I don't like spicy foods', are apt to become self-fulfilling prophesies. Instant resistance to a new experience is likely to represent a defence against new ideas and permit the persistence of a comfortable prejudice. But equally we know that the person who is too easily persuaded, who accepts the latest information without question, is in danger of being shallow, a flag blown hither and thither with every passing breeze, with neither character nor moral resolution. Excessive readiness to reshape one's way of thinking when presented with new ways of looking at things is just as morally reprehensible as remaining fixed in one's prejudices. And perhaps it is worth noting that many of our heroes and models of upright behaviour, from Job to Mandela via Nelson and Edison, were heroic mainly in their obstinate adherence to a principle and their willingness, either literally or metaphorically, to hold the telescope to their blind eye in order to avoid new information.

The process of education, therefore, involves a constant stream of decisions as to whether new experience should be incorporated into our store of knowledge, memories and patterned responses, or whether it should be rejected, downplayed or neglected. And if we decide to incorporate a new experience and the learning associated with it, this may or may not require very radical accommodation among the experiences and attitudes that we had previously decided to make part of our personality. Some new experiences may require a radical reassessment of everything that had come before, as might for example be the case in a religious conversion or adoption of a new political persuasion. Other new experiences may involve almost no accommodation, as when I learn a new word in a language which is not my main means of self-expression. The process of education is the process of building a personal history. It is an active process in which the individual chooses what is to be incorporated but also makes higher level decisions about how important each element is to be, or how much ambiguity or imprecision is acceptable in the personality as a whole.

There will be those who object to this characterization of experience as a process of choice; some experiences are so obtrusive, so invasive, that I cannot be said to have a choice as to whether I remember them or not. I cannot choose to remember or to forget my multiplication tables, which were drilled into me by a conscientious teacher at my primary school. I may not even be able to choose whether that was an enjoyable or hateful experience. But I am in a position to decide today where my understanding of basic arithmetic fits into the larger structure of knowledge with which I am trying to grapple, even at this moment. Nor can I choose to remember or forget the Alhambra in Granada. But I can decide whether that breath-taking building can just remain as an isolated experience of tourism, or whether it needs to be incorporated in some way into a broader cultural understanding.

Similarly, some teachers are unforgettable, whether for being inspirational or ogres, but only my subsequent actions, and my subsequent decisions how to deal with the knowledge they imparted, can decide whether they are a long-term influence on me, and, if so, whether for good or ill.

Those who object to the notion of choice in such a context tell me that they never had the experience of making a choice; they only did what was obvious and followed the expected path. And I can understand how that would be. However, I still argue that if the 'expected path' turned out to be objectionable, unpleasant or incompatible with other views they had of themselves, then at some point the individual on the expected path would rebel and choose a different route. We may not make conscious choices as to what we incorporate into our personalities, but at least in a negative sense we decide not to resist so long as the consequences of acquiescence are not too terrible.

In this sense, my choice to talk about education in terms of choice is a methodological decision. I believe that we can make sense of an individual's educational experiences if we view them as purposeful on the part of the learner. The learner is trying to accumulate a body of memories, dispositions and attitudes which produce a comfortable accommodation with their environment. (There are people who do not look particularly comfortable to me, in the sense that they take a hostile, aggressive or sceptical approach to everything around them, but my methodological assumption is that it must work for them, or they would change their approach.) This is ultimately a metaphysical position: that individuals select stances which are overall broadly of benefit to them, and that my first question, on seeing someone doing something that I would not do, should be, what benefit does this course of action bring them?

There may be cases where people literally have no choice. In a long career in teaching there have been two occasions on which I have felt it necessary to move away from an educational institution for my own health and sanity. In both cases I was so tired, worn down and lacking in energy that I felt that I was losing the ability to make decisions for my own benefit, so I left. In both cases I was fortunate enough to move to institutions which were educational in the broadest sense, and provided, for their staff as well as their students, an environment in which they could recuperate their energy, and, perhaps more importantly, develop a balanced perspective on their experiences. So I understand what it means to be in a situation where one's choices are limited, or possibly even at the point of disappearing. However, my methodological position suggests that we should treat all human behaviour as though it were a rational decision to select a route which produces benefits. If, at the end of all the research into education, we discover that there are some processes which cannot be understood in those terms, we will have identified an important area for further investigation. For the time being, therefore, let us see how far we can get with understanding education as a rational process of selecting the means for future benefit.

On any particular day, then, when I go into a class, probably something slightly over 50 per cent of those on the register will have decided to learn what I have decided to teach them. They will, however, have decided that what they learn is not going to make any great difference to their life; they will, if at all possible, keep the new knowledge in some watertight compartment of their memory until they have passed the examination, whereupon they anticipate that they will be able to jettison it safely. They may not have examined their decision very closely, and they might not describe their attitude exactly as I do, but their demeanour, and above all their limited commitment to my subject, will tell me that this is the overall effect of their approach. They are no trouble to me in class, they obtain decent results in their exams, and I wish them every success in their future. But I will not have made a major impact upon the way that they think about themselves or their world.

There is a second group who have decided not to learn what I have decided to teach them, but in whom the subject matter inspires no great emotion. They may decide to turn up for the class, or they may decide to absent themselves. They may decide to sit the final assessment after swotting up the material in the last few days, or they may drop out altogether. But overall they are no more trouble to me than the preceding group, and were it not for the fact that the government has decided to penalize the institution I work for if students do not complete their course, I would probably worry about this group of students as little as I do the previous group. They have made an instrumental choice about their learning which will probably work reasonably well in their context.

And then there is a third group of students, mercifully a small group and sometimes absent altogether, who have decided that they will not learn what I have decided to teach and actively reject it. They already have a mental framework in which they can accommodate their experience, and do not understand why I am trying to displace it with a new one which is more complicated, jargon-ridden, politically, religiously or morally objectionable, contrary to their experience, or in some other way requiring active resistance. This group of students can be fun, or very hard work, depending upon how energetic I feel at the time, and the degree of charm and humour with which they defend the barricades. (Richmond [2002: 59] has described something similar to the classification I have offered here, which she describes as a classification of 'resistance to coercion'.)

And finally there is the fourth (small) group of students, who have decided to learn what I want to teach, and have decided that it is important. They are going to incorporate new ways of thinking into their essential analytical frameworks, in much the same way as I did as I learned, and this is going to change the way in which they see the world. In a very real way, this is going to change their lives. These are the students who really motivate a teacher, the ones who make it worth getting up in the morning to be a teacher.

Other teachers have noticed these differences, of course. They have described surface learning and deep learning (which might roughly be equated with the view that the material itself is unimportant or important). But we need to be addressing ourselves to these questions in a more direct, and policy-related, way. For centuries it has been possible to develop a teaching strategy addressed only to the fourth group of students. I can turn up in the classroom and recite my notes in the dullest possible way, happy in the knowledge that this fourth group of students is going to learn anyway. No obstacle that I put in their way will deter them. They will go on to pass their exams, understand the subject, possibly become academics themselves and secure the future of the subject area. Government policy now means that we need to take a rather different view. If the second group of students is too large, we will lose funding. If the first group of students is too large, I am likely to be demoralized by confronting so many sponges happy to mop up information but with no real enthusiasm for being there.

The preferred way of dealing with this situation in policy terms is to try to identify the characteristics (or factors) which dispose a person to be a member of each of the four groups, in the hope that we can single out the students 'at risk of failure'. The second group of students are at risk of dropping out, and if we could identify them early (say from their poor attendance record) we could give them counselling or require their attendance, or give them additional exercises, in order to move them into the first group. The third group of students are exhibiting antisocial behaviour, and if we could only stuff them full of tranquillizers, or give them some work experience, we might be able to move them into the first or second group.

This approach suggests that there are some ways in which the students in each group differ, and their presence in one of the groups can be identified and then cured by some kind of 'magic bullet' or treatment on a quasi-medical model. This seems to me to be the most terrible nonsense. I spent most of my secondary education in the fourth group in lessons on maths and physics. I was in the first group for chemistry, the second group for geography and history. And I prefer not to think about the subjects that I was in the third group for.

The issue is one of priorities; one cannot be avidly interested in everything all at once. This is not a feature of my teachers, who, I am sure, were equally excellent in all subjects. Nor was it about my overall disposition to learning. It was about some choices that I was making at that time about what was important to me.

In general, the insight that students are active in generating their own learning is a position which is becoming increasingly acceptable and accepted. Under such general terms as constructivism, it is bolstered by the psychology of Vygotsky and/or Piaget, and is designed to promote the active engagement of learners. Further than that, it suggests that we need to engage directly and explicitly with the learning process as one of the areas of experience that the learner needs to understand. We need to give the learners the tools to manage their own learning, to decide whether deep or surface learning is appropriate to their current goal, to help them examine their own learning styles and develop strategies based upon their own strengths. I regard these as positive steps in the right direction.

But we need to go further than that. We need to understand whether there is anything that we can do to swell the numbers of the fourth group of students from 5 per cent of the student population to 10 per cent (at least we might start with a relatively modest goal). We might see whether there are changes that could be made that would move 10 per cent of the student population from the second group into the first group. And so on.

In another context I have stressed the idea that game-theory models have some distinct advantages in terms of describing situations of this sort (Turner 2004a). Game theory includes the concept of the mixed strategy, the idea that a homogeneous group of people in identical situations might nevertheless respond in entirely different ways. This is contrary to our commonsense understanding of education, which is generally based on the premise that if two groups of students respond to similar situations in very different ways there must be some identifiable characteristic (or factor) which would have allowed us to separate the two groups, if only we had known enough about them. For a number of reasons I prefer the game-theory notion that identical individuals might make different choices.

I shall return to those general philosophical reasons at various points in this book, but my main purpose in writing this book is to set out a framework for future policy-related research. In the following chapters I shall sketch out how game theory and related models can be used to describe educational settings in terms of purposeful choices made by the participants. These models will be elaborated so that a practical research programme could be developed.

Not to prejudge the issues involved, such a research programme, or the research projects that comprise it, would first of all test the extent to which an individual's choices could be viewed as reasonable and purposeful responses to their environment. But concrete research would also provide a range of information, the nature of which can, at this moment, only be open to speculation. As far as possible, some attempt will be made to suggest what conclusions empirical results might point to. However, the use of game-theory models, and in particular the idea of the mixed strategy, does have some profound implications for how we think about educational situations, whatever the empirical results, and these theoretical conclusions will also be highlighted.

This book, therefore, is designed to stand halfway between my earlier book (Turner 2004a) and fully developed research projects leading to empirical results that could inform policy. The aim and purpose of this book is to show how research could be designed to address a number of questions of prime importance to policy-makers.

Structure

My purpose in this book is to present a model of education as a complex system. In one way, explaining what a 'complex system' is will take the whole of the book. The weather is a complex system. Global events, such as El Niño, can have an effect upon weather patterns at a continental level, and are ultimately connected with the eddies of air which stir piles of leaves in my backyard. Different levels of the complex system are interconnected. But the interconnections are not rigid, or predictable with certainty. The weather is not a mechanism of clockwork, and I cannot work out the pattern of leaf-movements in my yard by looking at the movements of El Niño, or vice versa.

In the same way, to understand the complex system of education, we need to develop an understanding at different levels. We need to be able to understand the inner workings of the individual learner, their thinking processes and their motivation. This is an area which is traditionally covered by a subject called 'psychology'. We also need to be able to understand how individuals interact in small groups – in classrooms, in families and in planning committees. This is an area of concern we might expect to be studied in 'microsociology' or 'social psychology'. And we also need to be able to understand education in terms of policy direction, at the levels of institution and regional or national government. At this point we will be well into the subject of 'macrosociology'. We may even wish to put that understanding of education into an international setting, as part of a world-system approach. This may take our study into 'macroeconomics' or 'international studies'. This makes developing an understanding of education into a very ambitious project.

In order to have a complete understanding of educational systems, we need to be able to grasp the processes involved at all of those different levels. Yet, what happens in a classroom cannot be explained solely in terms of the psychology of the individuals involved. As one goes from class to class, one sees patterns of behaviour, or roles, repeated: the class clown, teacher's pet, swots and rebels, in-groups and out-groups can be found in every classroom, as though those roles were present in every group, waiting for the right person to fill them. Of course, it may help if the class clown is a bit overweight, wears glasses, and has learned to use humour to deflect animosity. But there is only room for one class clown in most classes. The social organization of the class is only loosely connected with the psychology of the individuals. It is this that makes a sociology of education necessary, as well as a psychology of education. The class starts to demonstrate properties and behaviours that are more than simply the sum of the individuals in the class. These are emergent properties.

And just as classes have emergent properties that are not properties of any of the individuals involved, so schools have emergent properties that are not necessarily properties of any of the classes in them, and national educational systems have emergent properties that are not properties of any of the schools that are part of them. For example, a 'mass system of education' is not a feature of any single school or class; it can only be seen when one looks at how all of the educational system is considered together, and how one school or institution relates to others.

Looked at in one way, this requirement to understand all the different levels of education at the same time, to see personal learning and national legislation as loosely connected but with neither one being reducible to the other, makes the study of education immensely complicated. On the other hand, it also offers some important clues as to how the question of researching education can be addressed. The idea that these different levels of understanding need to coexist without contradicting each other gives some valuable guidance as to the kind of theory that we are looking for. In Part 1 of this book (Theory) I will present those theoretical considerations that can help to build an understanding of education at all of these different levels.

Chapter 2 will present models from game theory, and illustrate how they can be used in developing an understanding of the interaction between individual motivation and preference and the operation of small groups. In the second part of this book I will go on to look at empirical research, practical settings and how game-theory models can be used to structure practical research projects and underpin policy. I think that the practical possibilities offered by such models are extremely important. But the most pressing reason for using such models is that they meet the basic theoretical requirements of the multilevel, complex system that I have described here. In game-theory models, the behaviour of groups is the outcome of the aggregation of individual preferences, but not in any simple way. Similarly, the behaviour of individuals is influenced by the group's setting, but not determined by it.

Game-theory models exhibit what I have described as multicentredness and partial autonomy. Multicentredness covers the notion that a group of identical people could be faced with identical choices, and yet different individuals might choose differently. Partial autonomy is the sense that the behaviour of educational systems at different levels − the individual, the class, the school, the national system − are linked without mutual determination. The presence of multicentredness secures partial autonomy. These theoretical aspects of game-theory models will be developed in Chapter 2.

Chapter 3 will develop the ideas of multicentredness up through the educational system, to institutional, national and international levels, using chaos or complexity theory. Chaos theory has the virtue of being compatible with game theory, in the sense that both leave scope for partial autonomy − the presence of similar patterns at different levels of organization, or 'recursive symmetries' as they are termed in complexity theory, is a central feature of complex systems, and more or less synonymous with what I have called partial autonomy. Similarly, game-theory models behave in complex and chaotic ways in certain circumstances. There may well be other and better models for understanding educational systems than the ones that I offer here, but the models presented in Chapters 2 and 3 have the virtue of being compatible with the basic theoretical requirement that the levels developed at different magnifications, as it were, at the microlevel and the macrolevel, do not contradict each other.

It should be clear by this point that the idea of theoretical modelling, or of developing intellectual models of human behaviour, is central to the structure of this book. But while theoretical models can be invaluable tools in the research process, they do also present the researcher with a number of temptations and pitfalls. The most pressing of these is the temptation to reify the models, to stop thinking of the models as convenient fictions and start thinking of them as a representation of reality.

It is interesting and stimulating to look at the learning of a pigeon, and to see how, in return for a structured reward programme, it can be taught to walk in a figure of eight pattern. It is even stimulating to think about the learning of human beings *as if* they were equivalent to pigeons, and to see the extent to which they learn when rewarded promptly. But it is a very different matter to conclude that the learning of human beings is equivalent to that of pigeons, and that all learning should be designed in behaviourist terms. The jump from viewing human learning *as if* it were the same as a pigeon's to acting on the assumption that it *is* the same as a pigeon's is the step at which a valuable theoretical model is reified and becomes a danger.

Education abounds in examples where the distinction between a model and its reification has been overlooked or forgotten. It is instructive to look at human behaviour *as if* it were motivated purely by economic gain (as I do in some sections of this book), but it is inexcusable to distribute all goods (including education) through market mechanisms on the assumption that human behaviour *is* motivated purely by economic gain. It is instructive to view students *as if* they had one of a small number of learning styles, but it is debilitating if we act on the assumption that each student *is capable of only one* learning style.

The educational literature is full of examples of good theoretical models that have been reified. This is then generally followed by a flurry of research articles that debunk the reification. The current round of critiques of learning styles is but one example. Piagetian stages of development, and the critiques of whether they really are universal, might be another. I have no particular quarrel with the use of theoretical models, nor with projects that debunk their reification. The cycle might be curtailed, however, if the over-enthusiasm that leads to their reification were tempered in the first place. Because of the importance of this question overall, I devote a whole chapter (Chapter 4) to the question of theoretical modelling: what it does involve and, in particular, what it does not involve.

One important feature of the use of models is that they shape what we can see and think about. We use theories and models to focus our attention or to skip over the commonplace. Changing the models that we use should, therefore, transform the way in which we think about practice, what we experience as professionals and what we look at as researchers. And that, in turn, should give us new insights and perceptions to shape our further practice. In the second part of this book, therefore, I turn my attention to practical concerns, and do three things in each of the chapters. First, I present a model of the educational phenomenon under review, taken from game theory and/or chaos theory. Secondly, I point to some evidence, either anecdotal or taken from the current research literature, that suggests that the new model may be a fruitful way of interrogating the behaviour that we see. And finally, I set out the areas where further research is necessary, and where the model presented raises questions that can only be addressed empirically.

For example, I have argued elsewhere (Turner 2004b) that education is better modelled as a traffic network, with interconnecting and crossing routes, rather than as a single ladder which one either ascends uniformly with those of one's own age, or drops out. The model is better, in part, because it is a game-theory/complexity-theory model that allows for the fact that different people will take different routes and their choices are not determined by the notion that there is one best route. The model is also better because it conforms with experiences that we have all had with pupils and students choosing educational directions that we thought were undesirable, or with students who have taken second or even third opportunities. But the model leaves a host of questions which remain unanswered. While educational researchers have been devoting their energies to identifying the factors that will help with the early identification of drop-outs, they have not been evaluating the competing incentives to follow the many different routes that are included in the new model. New research projects will be needed to answer those new questions.

This book, then, is a starting-point, not an end-point. In each of the chapters in the second part, a model will be presented. The model will be explored to indicate why it is a good model from a theoretical point of view. Some evidence will be sought in the current research literature to indicate that it might be a model that overcomes some of the known shortcomings of current research. But current research will not be able to answer questions that current researchers were not even asking. Each chapter will therefore set out a research programme for future research. And, of course, nobody can know what that future research might bring. The models presented here may need to be rejected or developed further.

The chapters in Part 2 (Practice) are divided by level: they address the micro-educational setting of the classroom, the operation of the national system or the global and globalized structure of education. The first (Chapter 5) addresses issues of classroom management. A multiperson game-theoretical model of the classroom is presented and tested against current research and anecdotal evidence. The model covers the behaviour of individuals where they are in a setting that is beyond their personal control but which is small enough to be influenced by their behaviour. Thus the atmosphere of the classroom cannot be decided exclusively by the action of one person, but whether one student chooses to listen attentively or send text messages to friends may affect the attitudes of others in the room, and hence the whole tone of the lesson.

Chapter 6 addresses the actions of individuals in still larger and less personal settings, such as the employment market. Their choices are shaped by the circumstances in which they find themselves, and the assumption that in some sense they are 'in competition' with peers, but the decision of any individual has minimal effect on the overall choices faced by others. This setting is modelled using two-person games against Nature.

Chapter 7 draws upon the insights from Chapters 5 and 6 to reflect upon the notion of equality of opportunity, and whether we need to think again about exactly what is meant by that phrase in the light of the models that have been presented. One of the constant difficulties in promoting equality of opportunity in the education system is that opportunity at any level is frequently limited by performance at an earlier level. We rarely know, however, whether this differentiated performance at an earlier level is the result of poor performance at a yet earlier level, some other kind of deficit such as a lack of understanding about how the system works or a lack of resources to invest, or a perfectly sensible choice in preparing for life after education, which will also be differentiated. Most of the models used in current research focus upon the first of these options, ever earlier antecedents of poor academic performance. Placing, alongside those, new models that can incorporate other possibilities may do little more than highlight how little we know about the mechanisms that may be operating here, but it certainly does help in examining what is meant by 'equality of opportunity'.

Having moved from the microlevel to the macrolevel, Chapter 8 returns to the microlevel once again, this time at the level of the individual and the psychology of learning. In Chapter 8 I examine the work of Lev Vygotsky. I argue that his description of the individual learning, as a person over-coming simple stimulus-response reactions by taking control over their own conditioning, and thereby gaining self-control, is compatible with the model of the person as a complex system. The result, which is, of course, anachronistic in the sense that Vygotsky could not have heard of complexity theory, nevertheless gives an elegant unity to our understanding of education, with the internal psychology of the learner mirroring educational phenomena at institutional, national and international levels.

That coherence between theoretical understandings at different levels is one of the goals that I have been aiming for, and hope that this book achieves. It is, however, difficult for me to judge how successful I have been, as coherence between the parts is not to be found in any of the parts. It is an emergent property of the larger system. But this unity of form and content is not simply something that I seek in a book about education, or in the models of education that I have presented; I believe that it is something that we should seek in the education system itself.

In contrast with this overall view of an education system as a loosely coupled, complex organization that leaves room for multicentredness on the part of participants, most current systems of quality assurance (as described in Chapter 9) are based upon a command-and-control structure and promulgate the belief that there is one best way to do things. The latter is frequently described as 'best practice'. In Chapter 9 I argue that such an approach to quality assurance is incompatible with much that has been described in the book, and is likely to prevent much more than it enables. It is not, generally, difficult to convert a complex system into a simple one. Since complex systems generally arise where there are multiple feedback loops and many centres of influence, simplicity can generally be produced by reducing the number of feedback loops and centralizing influence – results that command-and-control mechanisms are designed to achieve. However, the removal of complexity also removes all of those possibilities which arose along with complexity, among which I would see learning as central.

Chapter 9 analyses the application of quality assurance, and defines a new approach of 'good enough practice'.

Part 3 (Theory into Practice) contains only one chapter (Chapter 10) which brings together conclusions from the other sections of the book. Most importantly, these include a review of the links between the research models put forward and the possibility of developing research that can be used in the development of practical theory.

I can now see, however uncertainly, the links between the various aspects of theory and practice in education. The cross-connections are everywhere, and there is great difficulty in picking the right spot to begin. What I can see very clearly is the difficulty of conveying those cross-connections and that interrelationship in a text that is linear. I can only hope that the reader will grasp some of the possibilities that I hope it contains.

Part 1

Theory

Chapter 2

As Simple as Possible

This chapter will set out a range of lessons that can be learned from physical science, and particularly from the work of Albert Einstein, for the development of a social science of educational policy. It will argue that current approaches to research are simultaneously too simple and not simple enough. They are too simple in the sense that they are rooted in the assumption that all people of similar background or similar attitudes will respond to situations in a similar way. They leave no room for individual choice or for personal strategy. At the same time, they are too complicated, in that they suggest that we should be able to predict the behaviour of each individual. The latter is, strictly speaking, unnecessary; knowing how many people will choose a particular route through the education system is more useful than knowing which people they will be.

Various websites quote Albert Einstein as having said, 'Things should be as simple as possible, but no simpler', or something similar. There is an interesting methodological injunction here towards simplicity, a kind of latter-day Occam's razor, that only concepts which are essential to an explanation should be included in that explanation. At the same time, there is the hint that one can go too far, can try to understand complex situations without quite enough conceptual subtlety. In his search for simplicity, first in relativity and later in a unified field theory, Einstein sought to create an understanding which was as simple as possible. His ultimate frustration was that he recognized that artificial simplicity was of no value, and that a successful theory needed to be complex enough to cover the important features of the world that he wanted to describe.

Obviously, in deciding that one particular description is as simple as possible but another is excessively simplified, one is not coming to a conclusion that can be arrived at by immediate apprehension, without going into long and difficult research. So in examining whether Einstein's dictum can be of any value in the development of policy-related research in education studies, it might be as well to take a broader view of Einstein's work and see whether there is anything more that he has to offer us in terms of understanding our project.

In his popular exposition of relativity, Einstein (1920) sets out for the interested lay-person the key elements of the theory of relativity. Although relativity is clearly a sophisticated theory, in that work he seeks to set out in non-mathematical terms the key issues so that they can be understood outside the narrow circle of professional mathematical physicists. If nothing else, this suggests that Einstein thought there was something of general importance that we could all learn from the processes of theoretical physics.

The structure of the argument, as set out in the first 20 pages of that book, is extremely elegant. Einstein considers a physical situation, a train travelling along a railway embankment past a light signal. After setting out some basic principles of measurement, he sets out to ask what the speed of light is from the perspective of a passenger on the train. There are two possibilities: (1) the speed of light is c for all observers, and therefore c for the passenger on the train, or (2) the speed of light is $c + v$, the speed of the train being added to the speed of light relative to the embankment, to give the speed of light for the passenger on the train. Even without going out and performing a single experiment, we now know that physics is in deep trouble. We can, with Einstein's help, imagine a situation in which two different principles of physics can be brought to bear, to arrive at two contradictory conclusions as to the state of affairs. One or other of the two principles must be abandoned.

Now consider an educational setting. A child works his way through a mathematics test, and achieves a particular score. How should we understand that score? Should we (1) regard it as an outcome of the effort that the child has put in and give him praise for a high mark or blame him for a low mark, or (2) explain it in terms of his inherited intelligence, family background variables, schooling variables, etc., and therefore simply see it as an outcome of his background for which no praise or blame is due? And if a student complains that he worked much harder than a fellow student who received a better score on the test, is that a legitimate complaint or a red herring?

The problem is that we have two entirely different frameworks of reference that we can bring to bear on educational settings. In the latter, which is supported by the vast bulk of educational research, educational outcomes are the almost mechanical outcome of background variables, and no praise or blame is due. In the other framework, the moral and ethical practice of education which most of us inhabit day-to-day, educational outcomes are the result of personal effort, and students are to be praised for success and blamed for failure. The fact that we have two frameworks or principles that we can bring to bear with contradictory results is not the answer. It should, however, be the start of the question. It should point to the fact that something is wrong and needs to be addressed directly, in much the same way as Einstein demonstrated that the parallel problem in physics showed that something needed to be done. Either one framework of description or the other needs to be abandoned, or both, in order to strengthen a framework in which such contradictory accounts are no longer possible.

Perhaps it should be noted that this is not an esoteric or remote theoretical issue. Dweck (2000: 62–3) describes an experiment conducted by her and a co-researcher (Mueller and Dweck 1997) and another related study. College students were invited to decide who should be admitted to a university programme: students with high examination marks, but poor marks for effort and course-work, or students with low examination marks but good marks for effort and course-work. In the general setting that Dweck describes, students were being asked to select either (1) on some background determined and fixed indicator which can broadly be described as intelligence, or (2) on something more like personal effort. Mueller and Dweck concluded that people divide in their preferences on the issue, broadly in line with their view of what sort of thing intelligence is.

This is the area where university admission tutors make decisions all the time. Perhaps more importantly, this is the area where university admissions tutors in the UK will be held to account by an Office for Fair Access to Higher Education, but where the ground-rules for understanding the process and theorizing the outcomes are completely inadequate. How do we compare the worthiness of a candidate from a comprehensive school in an inner-city area with a candidate from a private school in the suburbs, when we have no unified theory of performance, background and effort? We need improved theory in this area for very practical reasons, and the parallel with Einstein's description of the state of physics in the late nineteenth century is striking. The stimulus to improved theoretical frameworks for this area of education is in our hands, even if the answers are not.

Perhaps it should be noted at this point that there is a very clear resolution of this problem, which comes under the general heading of cultural relativism; the child from the suburbs and the child from the inner city have been inducted into different cultures. Their performances are qualitatively different, incomparable or incommensurate, and therefore cannot be reduced to a simplistic measure such as examination grades. Cultural relativism has some intellectual standing, some of it derived by reflected glory from the theory of relativity, and the notion that cultural relativism is in some way the social sciences' answer to relativity. Cultural relativism derives from the fact that observers cannot make purely objective measurements; making a measurement can itself influence that which is being measured. And certainly, in education, anybody who doubts that the presence of an examination (measurement of performance) has an impact upon motivation and performance itself obviously needs to have a rethink. However, relativity is actually something very different from relativism.

As Einstein (1920: 99) describes it: 'The general principle of relativity requires that all these [frames of reference] can be used as reference-bodies with equal laws of nature; the laws themselves must be quite independent of the choice of [frame of reference].' Far from being a vindication of cultural relativism, relativity is a methodological injunction that the laws of nature should be the same for all observers, and that, therefore, we should do everything possible to avoid cultural relativism. Cultural relativism is an invitation to have two or more theoretical accounts of a single physical situation, and no way of choosing between them; relativity is an injunction to go beyond that situation and to seek to frame explanations in such a way that only one can be applied to a physical situation. This may suggest, in turn, that we are in need of theories in the social sciences that are more reflexive, more abstract than the ones that we have available to us at the current time. In short, it suggests that we have erred a little too far in the direction of the simple, to the extent of having theories that are currently simpler than possible.

Of course, there is a legitimate point to be made when the cultural relativist argues that a whole human experience cannot be reduced to a single examination grade, or even a number of examination grades. The richness of human experience and individuality cannot be reduced to three grade As at A-level, and the proud possessors of those three grade As are equivalent only to that one, and very limited, extent. But if we leave the matter at that point, we may be very fine educational researchers, but we are justifiably the complete despair of policy-makers. We need to develop a practical sense of whether a student who has top examination marks but is rejected by a university course is being treated fairly or not, because unless we can deal with that question, many of our other aspirations cannot be achieved.

There are those who will argue that this uniqueness of human experience signals the end of any hope that we might have for applying scientific methods in the social sciences in general and in the study of education in particular. But we need to remember that scientific method is simply a method of abstracting a narrow range of relevant features and concentrating on those at the expense of others. Nor is it exclusively a method of science. We classify objects as the same whenever we use a noun in speech. Thus Jupiter, Saturn, Venus, Mars and the Earth are all planets, but this does not begin to cover the range of differences from the turbulent and dense atmosphere of Jupiter, to the life-supporting Earth. Kepler's laws of planetary motion abstract only the mass of the planets to demonstrate that they all travel in ellipses, and this is done without taking into account the singularity of the experience of standing in a tropical rainforest or of walking along the Pennine Way. When we group objects together we concentrate on those similarities and differences which are relevant to our classification. Blake complained of Newton that by treating all objects as composed of point-masses, he had removed colour and singular experience from the world and left a drab and abstract construction. And of course, in one way this is true. We could not hope through a similar process of abstraction to capture the subjective richness of human experience, but that would not be the objective.

We flatter ourselves that the reason that human experience cannot be reduced to such abstractions is that, compared with the material world of point-masses, the social world is too complicated. The exact opposite is true. The material world, in spite of the richness that Blake noted, appears simple because we have the abstraction of point-masses developed by Newton. The social world appears complex beyond imagining because, up to this point, we have failed to produce a corresponding abstraction in the social sphere. We need to be able to distinguish between an abstraction and the reality it purports to describe.

We have not necessarily been very good at drawing this distinction. There is the world of difference between 'The concept of a market, and the processes of market exchanges, can be used as a tool to bring order to our understanding of human action', and 'Human interactions constitute a market'. But the two are frequently confused, and people think that it is in some way demeaning to use the concept of a market to understand human behaviour, because it cannot take into account higher human purposes, such as compassion and altruism. In fact, of course, the concept of a market can be used to analyse human behaviour, and by showing how much behaviour can be understood (and by implication how much cannot be understood) in terms of market forces, it shows us more clearly how much is due to other forces, such as those higher moral purposes.

It is a smaller but equally reprehensible step when the jump is made from 'Human interactions constitute a market', to 'We ought to organize our institutions as markets'. The result is that policy becomes intimately but incorrectly linked with theory.

What I am doing here is suggesting that we use a model of economic activity as a conceptual tool for understanding the behaviour of people. Those people are assumed to be *Homo economicus*: that is to say, they are assumed to be able to put a cash value on their utilities (the value they place on consuming goods and services) and on their own labour, and are expected to act so as to increase (although not necessarily maximize – this is a point to which I shall return later) their own benefits. This comes under the general heading of making things as simple as possible.

I would hardly need to add that this does not mean leaping to the conclusion that all commodities should be distributed according to market principles, were it not the case that this gulf had already been stupidly leapt on numerous occasions in the past, suggesting the beneficial consequences of market disciplines on schools, nurseries, hospitals and transport systems, using voucher schemes, tax rebates, private–public partnerships and scholarships. There are many things which should not be allocated according to the regulation of market forces: life, liberty, the pursuit of happiness, the franchise, and legal advice when charged with a crime are among the things which have to be allocated so that every person has an equal claim to them quite independently of economic considerations. Which commodities can safely be allocated through the market and which cannot is one of the questions which should be addressed through policy-related research. It is not one of the answers that we should have *before* we embark on said research.

What I am arguing here is that the use of *Homo economicus* as a conceptual tool is well suited to exploring human interactions, with a view to establishing which actions can be understood in terms of market forces and which cannot. We can hope to develop policy which will take into account the disruptive effect of organizing areas of activity along market lines when they cannot be understood as a market, just as much as we can hope to introduce market discipline into areas where interactions can be understood as a market. In this way we can hope to avoid much of the nonsense of current free-market dogma, which certainly falls into the category of being simpler than is possible.

The other area where we can avoid being simpler than possible is in our understanding of groups. The whole logic of large-scale survey techniques is based upon the idea that if we could identify homogeneous groups of individuals, then we would expect them all to behave in the same way. *Ceteris paribus*, other things being equal, those distinguishing characteristics that allowed us to identify the separate nature of those homogeneous groups would explain why one group behaved one way rather than another.

Education studies are full of attempts to develop this kind of explanation. The search for intelligence, either general intelligence, *g*, or multifaceted factors of intelligence, whether inherited from parents or learned from teachers, have been identified as ways of explaining different levels of performance. Those who have this magic quality do well at school, those who lack it do not. Even emotional intelligence, which at least represents a branching-out into less tangible fields of development, is couched in terms of the dominant discourse of intelligence, the mystery factor which explains school performance.

Whatever cannot be explained by intelligence might be explained by the wealth of the child's father, the upward social aspirations of its mother, the number of siblings, the presence of books in the home, the language patterns of significant adults, the qualifications of its teachers, birth-weight, the parents' smoking habits or a telephone at home, to name but a few candidates which have been tried. Each failure simply stimulates the next attempted explanation.

If this approach worked, then using a multidimensional array we would be able to identify a group of young people identical on all of these variables and any others we chose to add, and we would expect all members of a homogeneous group to perform equally well in school, and differently from the members of any other group. In short, we should be able to define clearly separate groups in which there was no variance of performance. This would be the ideal outcome of most large-scale survey methods of analysing school performance in terms of background variables. However, this general model again comes under the heading of being more simple than possible. Whenever we divide people into groups using one group of criteria, we normally discover that there is more within group variance on unrelated criteria than there is between group variance using those criteria. In short, no practical attempt to divide people into groups on such a basis has ever been successful.

One further point should perhaps be made. If it had proved possible to perform such a multivariate analysis successfully, then a byproduct of that process would be that we would know the outcome of the educational process for each individual, simply from knowing which group they belonged to. The knowledge we had of the independent variables, used for grouping learners into homogeneous groups, would predetermine the educational performance of each member of those groups. It is this feature that leaves no room for the exercise of decision or determination by the individuals. It is this feature which means that the two different frames of reference that we are trying to apply come into conflict. And it is this feature of our current explanatory theories which points to the fact that there is an irreconcilable difficulty at the heart of the research process as it is currently understood.

It could be otherwise. What I am going to argue over the course of this book is that models derived from game theory avoid these difficulties. In particular, game theory contains the notion of a 'mixed strategy', which is to say the notion that a homogeneous group of individuals faced with identical choices might be expected, under specific circumstances, to behave in very different ways. The corollary of this is that if we observe an outcome in which members of a group all decide to perform in a similar way, we would not be in a position to deduce that group has something in common that explains their similar decision. They would simply be those sections of different homogeneous groups who happened to coincide in their choice. The simplest way of explaining how this might work is probably to give an example from game theory which illustrates the important points.

In the archetypical 'game' described by game theory, two players each have to make a decision unobserved by the other player. Depending upon the combination of the decisions made by the two players, one or other of them is decided to be the winner, and the loser pays the winner some previously agreed forfeit. The children's game of Scissors, Paper, Stone is therefore a game of this type. Each player makes a decision as to which hand-shape to display on the count of three; they therefore make their choices in ignorance of the other player's choice. If both players make the same choice, the play is void and is replayed. In any other case, when the players make different choices, the winner is well defined according to the schema:

> Paper beats Stone
> Stone beats Scissors
> Scissors beat Paper.

The winning player gains one point: the losing player loses one point. The winner's gains are therefore equal to the loser's losses.

For obvious reasons, such a game is called a two-person zero-sum game. It is the simplest form of game which illustrates the important points set out above. If ever you meet a player of this game who consistently plays only one option, Paper for example, you know that you have met somebody who has not properly understood the game. As soon as a player's selections are predictable, then they are likely to lose to an opponent who can anticipate their choices. A person who understands the game would be expected to play each of the three options with equal frequency, but in a randomized order that made prediction as difficult as possible.

The structure of the game can be represented in a pay-off matrix, which shows how much Player A wins, and therefore how much Player B loses, when they make specific choices. This pay-off matrix is shown in Figure 2.1.

Now let us introduce a simple modification to the standard game; let us suppose that we make a win for A much more valuable where Player A chooses Stone and Player B chooses Scissors. We might make this worth four times as much as a normal win. The resulting pay-off matrix can be shown in Figure 2.2.

I will come to formal solutions of games later, but we can anticipate what effect this change will have on the way the game is played simply by

		Choice of Player A		
		Scissors	Paper	Stone
	Scissors	0	−1	+1
Choice of Player B	Paper	+1	0	−1
	Stone	−1	+1	0

Figure 2.1 Simple pay-off matrix for 'Scissors, Paper, Stone'

		Choice of Player A		
		Scissors	Paper	Stone
	Scissors	0	−1	+4
Choice of Player B	Paper	+1	0	−1
	Stone	−1	+1	0

Figure 2.2 Modified pay-off matrix for 'Scissors, Paper, Stone'

considering the benefits to each player and assuming that both players understand the nature of the game they are in, behave as logically as possible to maximize their winnings, and assume that the other player is doing the same. These are the basic assumptions that people make choices after the fashion of *Homo economicus*, which are built into game theory. It will be important to come back and examine these assumptions later, but for the present we can examine the operation of a game-theory model.

At first sight, it would appear that Stone had just become a very attractive option for Player A. However, by the same token, Scissors has just become a very unattractive option for Player B. If Player B stops playing Scissors altogether, to avoid the large loss when this choice coincides with Player A choosing Stone, the two players are then in a different game, with a reduced pay-off matrix, as shown in Figure 2.3.

For Player A, the choice of Paper is now always better than the choice of Stone; from A's perspective, when Player B chooses Paper, a draw is better than a loss, and when Player B chooses Stone, a win is better than a draw. Thus for Player A, Paper is always better than Stone, or, in the language of game theory, the choice of Paper 'dominates' the choice of Stone. If we leave out the choice which is dominated, a choice which it makes no sense for Player A to select, we are left with a further reduced pay-off matrix, as shown in Figure 2.4.

		Choice of Player A		
		Scissors	Paper	Stone
Choice of Player B	Paper	+1	0	−1
	Stone	−1	+1	0

Figure 2.3 Reduced pay-off matrix for 'Scissors, Paper, Stone'

		Choice of Player A	
		Scissors	Paper
Choice of Player B	Paper	+1	0
	Stone	−1	+1

Figure 2.4 Further reduced pay-off matrix for 'Scissors, Paper, Stone'

Paper cannot be described as an attractive choice for Player B, as the best outcome is a draw and the worst a loss on that selection. However, Player B cannot afford only to play Stone, or in that case Player A can always win by playing Paper. We would therefore expect to see both players randomizing their choices with A playing Paper more frequently than Scissors and B playing Paper more frequently than Stone. (If this last step is not clear, it is not terribly important as I shall deal with the formal solution of two-person non-zero-sum games of this type at a later point.)

Now, going back to the first step, the disincentive for Player B to play Scissors was not absolute; the particular loss only had a value of −4 to Player B, not −1,000 or −1,000,000. We might therefore anticipate that Player B would very occasionally play Scissors, and that Player A might therefore find it advantageous to add the occasional choice of Stone into his or her strategy. Overall, therefore, we might expect that in any sequence of ten plays, Player A might choose Paper on six occasions, Scissors on three and Stone on one, while Player B might choose Paper on six occasions, Stone on 3 and Scissors on one.

There is an interesting counterintuitive aspect to this analysis. We started from the assumption that making a particular win much more attractive for Player A would make the choice associated with that big win more attractive. However, having followed through the logic of the game and arriving at an informal solution, we have discovered that, in fact, the choice associated with a big win is likely to be played much less frequently. Rather than trying to maximize their gains in a naïve way, the players are trying to minimize the gains of the other. Within that framework of assumptions, they are then trying to maximize their own gains on the assumption that their opponent is trying to minimize them. Game theory has developed the concept of 'maximin' options to characterize this behaviour.

Now, with only one more flight of fancy, the importance of such a game-theory approach can be seen very clearly. Imagine a school playground with 100 pairs of children playing our modified game of Scissors, Paper, Stone. And further assume that the informal solution of this game set out above is accurate, and that at one instant all 100 pairs make one play, and that 200 children select either Scissors, or Paper, or Stone. If we freeze that moment and look around the playground we would anticipate that on average 40 children will have made the selection of Scissors.

How shall we account for the fact that on that single play 40 children chose Scissors? Should we look for the distinguishing feature that makes them all the same, that gives them something in common? Should we search for the personality factor that predisposes them to choosing Scissors? From the way that this model has been set up, we know that we should do no such thing. The group of 40 children selecting Scissors is made up of two quite different groups. From a homogeneous group of 100 children who are taking the part of Player A, 30 will have chosen Scissors. And from a homo-geneous group of 100 who are taking the part of Player B, 10 will have chosen Scissors.

The features of this model are striking. A group that is homogeneous in its make-up and faces identical choices may nevertheless be expected to make very different choices. And a group that is homogeneous in terms of out-comes may nevertheless have faced different incentives and different choices. The model does not assume a simple link between independent vari-ables and dependent variables.

Perhaps more importantly, the model does not tell us very much at all about the choices of individuals. In the next play of Scissors, Paper, Stone, we would expect another group of 40 children to select Scissors, but we would not expect them to be the same individuals. If we wished to attach approval or opprobrium to the choice of Scissors, there would still be the opportunity to assign praise or blame for the choice. We would not be right, however, to think that those taking the part of Player A were more virtuous (or villainous, as the case may be) because three times as many of them had chosen Scissors; that was a consequence of the reward system that we had established.

Game-theory models permit us to separate the overall description of group behaviour from accounts of individual choices. In doing this they overcome the major difficulty that I identified with theory in relation to educational research. By separating the description of the group from the description of the individual, we can no longer bring to bear on a single situation the two separate models of behaviour – the group disposition and the individual choice. We have avoided the difficulties that arise from being more simple than possible.

It should perhaps be noted that in general, in the real world, it is much easier to anticipate the behaviour of groups than to anticipate the behaviour of individuals. I can be fairly sure that in term-time, at half past eight on a Monday morning, there will be a queue of traffic for the car park on campus. I might even have a fairly good guess as to how many cars would be in that queue. But if I was asked to guess which colleagues would be in that traffic jam next Monday, I would have to start trying to guess which colleagues might be working off-campus, which might have made a special effort to get in early and beat the rush, which had appeared to me to be incubating flu, and so on. The number of considerations that might affect an individual choice can be extended more or less indefinitely.

But from the point of view of the policy-maker, which individuals are involved is frequently completely immaterial. They need to know how many parking places to allocate, how to organize the traffic flow, how many applications they can expect for the degree in chemistry, what proportion of candidates that we offer places to can be expected to turn up for the programme. Policy-makers are nearly always interested in group behaviour rather than individual behaviour. So long as we use models for research that tie group and individual behaviour together, then we have the paradox that free will seems impossible, and that policy-makers can intervene inappropriately in individual cases. Once we see the possibility of using models that separate group and individual behaviour, a whole new range of research opens up. Not the least attractive among the future directions that research might take is a meaningful investigation of concepts that are as ubiquitous as they are nebulous – equality of opportunity, fair access, affirmative action, mitigation, and so on.

At first sight, game-theory models no doubt seem to be complicated and in conflict with Einstein's dictum that things should be as simple as possible. However, if we consider the range of philosophical benefits that such models appear to offer, then we might indeed come to the conclusion that they are as simple as possible, and that our main difficulties have arisen from the fact that up to this point we have tried to apply models that are too simple.

In particular, game-theory models and complexity-theory models are the simplest models which I have found that can incorporate the notion that a homogeneous group of people faced with an identical decision might nevertheless make different choices. I have called this feature of those models multicentredness, and it captures the idea that there is more than one good route through life's choices. The alternative view, that a homogeneous group will always respond to the same decision in the same way, or that there is one best way of doing things, I have called single-centredness. The corollary of single-centredness is that if we observe a population dividing over a decision, then we should be able to identify that which separates the two groups – an underlying cause.

My contention is that education must be understood as a multicentred process, and that the simplest theories that can accommodate that requirement are those that I advance in this book. Game theory and complexity theory therefore meet the requirement of being as simple as possible but no simpler; all extant, single-centred theories of education fall foul of the prescription not to be too simple.

The exact way in which these insights can be developed, and turned into practicable research projects, will form the basis of the rest of this book.

Chapter 3

An Arrow into the Air

I shot an arrow into the air,
It fell to earth, I knew not where;
For, so swiftly it flew, the sight
Could not follow it in its flight.

I breathed a song into the air,
It fell to earth, I knew not where;
For who has sight so keen and strong,
That it can follow the flight of song?

Long, long afterward, in an oak
I found the arrow, still unbroke;
And the song, from beginning to end,
I found again in the heart of a friend.
(Henry Wadsworth Longfellow, 'The Arrow and the Song')

Introduction

I take it to be the case that everything that is really important in the educational process cannot be controlled. I find Vygotsky's description of a two-stage or two-cycle process of learning to be completely persuasive. In the first cycle the teacher presents and makes public a conceptual framework, a range of guided experiences, a set of mental tools and/or appropriate evidence. This process can be fully structured and controlled; it is what teachers can do best. But once that first cycle is complete, the really important part of learning takes place within the learner. New ideas have to be evaluated, feelings about the new experiences recognized, values attached to the new learning and very possibly old mental frameworks adjusted to accommodate the new. And all of that second cycle is beyond the reach and the control of the teacher.

Like the action of firing an arrow into the air, or the breathing of a song into the air, the activity can itself be infinitely finely crafted, and yet the eventual landing place can be quite unknown. In this sense, all teachers are breathing their songs and lessons into the air.

The learning process involves those basic elements of complexity which are described by complexity theory or chaos theory. The process, as has been noted here, is unpredictable. This is partly because it is quite literally out of control. Obviously, from the point of view of the teacher, the learning process is beyond their control, as the learner is ultimately responsible not only for learning but also for what is learnt. The teacher may present a lesson on the history of the Tudors, while the learner may learn a lesson in politics, in the reading of human character, in the theory of pedagogy, or in the passing of clandestine messages. But neither is the learner completely in control of the learning process. What we learn, and more particularly the significance of what we learn, may not become clear to us until many years after the event. In that sense the learning process as a whole cannot be planned in the ordinary way.

But more specifically, what happens in any particular learning incident is highly sensitive to the initial conditions. Teachers are urged to take account of 'where their pupils are coming from', but in practice this can be done only in the clumsiest of ways. Where a pupil is coming from might be the concrete operational stage, an argument with a friend or parent, or a disappointing performance on the football pitch. Indeed, it might be all three, and the teacher can hardly know which is the most important to come to terms with. The learning process is highly susceptible to the circumstances in which it starts, but the full texture of that environment is unknowable.

However, the learning process is not simply out of control. The really interesting thing about learning is that learning and understanding involve many nested layers. When I read a poem I am aware of the way letters on the page represent spoken sounds, I follow the literal meaning of the flow of words, I remember past incidents and facts, and I reflect on life and love and the meaning of life. But these are only loosely connected with each other, and only the lowest level can be brought under control. A teacher can (my teachers did) make me learn poems by heart, recite them out loud and conduct detailed analysis of their construction. But the memories that are recalled and the emotions aroused cannot be commanded, not even by me. The mechanics of reading and the memorization by heart do not necessarily add up to produce the overall impact of a poem, any more than my understanding of science is the sum total of all the exercise problems that I have ever solved. This feature of having a whole which cannot be defined entirely through the definition of its parts is called emergence, and is another feature of complex systems.

Finally, the learning process involves numerous feedback loops. As we try to learn, we monitor our own thinking processes in order to make fine adjustments and corrections. We may also enjoy the benefit of detailed feedback from a teacher. And when we have eventually mastered some new area of skill or knowledge, the chances are that we will want to display it publicly so that we can receive feedback from a wider audience (until we discover that a wider audience is not interested, in which case most of us learn to keep quiet).

These four characteristics are typical of complex and chaotic systems: unpredictability, sensitivity to initial conditions, emergent properties and multiple feedback loops. Taken together they might be said to define what it is for a system to be complex or chaotic. This appears at first sight to mark out teaching as an activity which is doomed to failure. If the outcome of teaching cannot be predicted, if we cannot be sure where the process will end up, it would seem that teachers may be involved in an activity which is as likely to be harmful as benign. What is left for teachers to do? And what can research add to a fundamentally unpredictable process? To address these questions we need to step aside for a moment from the specifics of the learning process and examine some aspects of complex systems which will inform the metaphor.

Complex systems

The concept of complex systems is a mathematical model, or metaphor, for how actual systems behave. The value of that metaphor is that the abstract mathematical model can be developed so that particular features can be emphasized. These features can then be used to highlight, classify and predict features of the behaviour of actual systems. The value of the metaphor is that it brings attention to bear upon specific features of actual systems. This is also the weakness of a metaphor in the sense that it may focus attention on aspects which are not of primary importance or may lead us to suppose that the metaphor encompasses all aspects of real systems. One always has to be wary of whether a metaphor is leading to false assumptions being made, when the metaphor is stretched beyond the range within which it is a useful description of the events under consideration.

What needs to be understood is that terms such as 'chaos' or 'complexity' are not naturally occurring phenomena; they are constructed out of a range of appropriate theories, and they give very specific meaning, not necessarily a commonsense meaning, to a range of technical terms. Much the same happened in the late-nineteenth century with the term 'random'. The behaviour of roulette wheels, dice, tosses of a coin and gas molecules are supposed to be random, but this does not mean that no patterns can be discerned in the behaviour of those objects. On the contrary, the formalization of the notion of 'random' made it possible to see significant patterns in the way that roulette wheels and dice behave. And these concepts could then be extended to natural events, such as gas molecules and kicking horses, to gain an improved understanding of events which had hitherto defied accurate description.

In the same way, chaos theory or complexity theory does not stop at the thought that some events are complex, but goes beyond that to develop a model of what it means for a system to be complex, and how we might expect chaotic systems to behave. Ironically, systems that are relatively simple, or at least can be specified relatively simply, can exhibit complex behaviour. Four of the characteristics of complex systems have been identified in the introduction to this chapter: unpredictability, sensitivity to initial conditions, emergent properties and feedback loops. These can be illustrated in a relatively simple example.

Figure 3.1 shows a pattern known as the Sierpinski Triangle. It can be produced in a three-step process, repeated many times. The starting figure is a black, right-angled, isosceles triangle, and the three steps are as follows:

1. Make a right-angled, isosceles, triangular figure by combining three copies of the original figure around a triangular space.

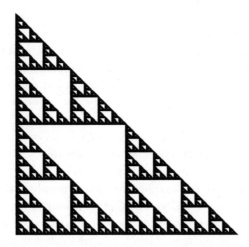

Figure 3.1   Sierpinski Triangle

2. Reduce this new triangular figure to half its size.
3. Replace the original figure with the new one and start again.

The process of feedback loops is illustrated in the very way that the creation of this figure is described. It is produced by repeatedly operating in the same way on the figure which results from the previous iteration.

However, the process of emergence can also be seen in the fact that the new figure is quite literally indescribable. Each time the figure is reduced to half its size (reduced to a quarter of its area) and is copied three times, the figure should need only three-quarters of the ink that was needed in the iteration before. The figure should become ever lacier, until it takes no ink at all to print it, and Figure 3.1 would be a blank. And yet the figure is plainly neither a blank, nor a black triangle, but something which is easily apprehended as something in between, without being easily described.

On the other hand, the unpredictability which arises in the context of Figure 3.1 is clear if I say that I am going to throw a dart at the figure with the intent that the point should penetrate a piece of paper that has ink on it. In those areas where there is ink at all, the black and the white are so interlinked as to make it impossible to tell whether the dart will land in black paper or white. Moreover, since magnifying any part of the figure will simply produce a figure which is identical to the whole, there is no way that more detailed information, more refined measurement, can improve my chances of striking a black part of the pattern. The smallest error, the slightest twitch when launching the dart, may result in the outcome that was not desired.

As the Sierpinski Triangle illustrates, perhaps a little too well, emergence does not simply mean that patterns at different levels of magnification are different from each other – they are also similar to each other. In more complex patterns, such as the Mandelbrot set, there are similarities in the pattern, but the smaller patterns are not strict repeats of the larger pattern. However, there is something about the various patterns that can be identified as a family resemblance.

Complexity as metaphor

Having taken this brief diversion into the formal world of fractals and chaos theory, it is time to return to thinking about educational institutions. Using complexity as a metaphor, a number of common insights into the way in which schools and colleges operate can be brought together into a more general scheme. Patterns of behaviour tend to be reflected through the institution at different levels. If the head bullies his or her senior staff, that tends to be reflected in a culture of bullying that is repeated with variations through the school, right up to the settling of disputes in the playground. On the other hand, if the head is supportive and polite, this too can be reflected at all levels throughout the school. Schools have a pervasive culture which is difficult to put one's finger on precisely, but which is found in the family resemblances between the behaviours of different members of the community.

This tendency for patterns of behaviour has been noted in cycles of victim-becomes-bully and abused-becomes-abuser, but complexity theory takes us beyond any simple, mechanical understanding of such phenomena. Indeed, complexity theory suggests that the cyclical patterns are properties of the system, rather than personal characteristics of either bully or victim. One can have a personal commitment to spreading happiness and light in the organization, but if at every turn one meets grumpiness and ill-humour, one's resolve is likely to slacken.

A systemic approach therefore tends to be rather more optimistic about the possibility for change and personal growth. Taking a bully out of a cultural environment which supports bullying, and putting him or her into a culture that does not, can be expected to bring about change – not necessarily with certainty or with immediate effect, but in the medium-term.

In contrast with this notion of loosely connected levels of organization which have a reciprocal impact on each other, educational institutions today tend to be dominated by a culture of accountability. Accountability thrives upon an organizational structure that stresses line management, and the ability of a line manager to receive detailed accounts of what subordinates have done. An accountability culture introduces audit trails, inspections, standardized tests and endless bureaucracy, so that the successes of the system can be recorded. The watchword of the accountable institution is 'control'.

Again, accountability shows a distinct tendency to permeate a whole organizational culture, and to be repeated at different levels in the organization. If the head seeks to monitor the activities of senior staff, and the activity of senior staff is to monitor and control the work of junior staff, the flow of bureaucratic controls through the organization will be inexorable.

As I have noted when discussing games against Nature (Chapter 6), this imperative to control has been fuelled by a parallel reinterpretation of the notion of risk, indeed a misrepresentation of the notion of risk. When I was a schoolboy, young people were exposed to risk in the certain knowledge that there might be negative results, but that in the absence of risk there could not be positive results. There were occasional tragedies: a school friend died in a mountaineering accident, and the brother of a friend was killed in a road accident. These extreme tragedies were matched by a greater number of broken bones and gaping wounds, and we all ended up in the accident and emergency unit of the local hospital sooner or later.

I have no idea what the benefits of being exposed to all those risks were, and I suspect that is because I take them for granted. The freedom to wander around a big city from a relatively early age, to be able to cycle off for a day's exploring, or to go camping where one learned to cook or went hungry, probably helped to form a character that I am proud of, whatever anybody else says. But a precise link between risks and benefits is hard to define. (Notice that even here I am slipping into the modern usage of 'risk' to mean the opposite of 'benefits'.)

I remember my childhood not as being an arena for control, but, on the contrary, as being a time when my parents made very specific and difficult decisions, against their inclinations, to relinquish control. I remember the decision (taken reluctantly) to let my brothers and I have bicycles, and another (taken less reluctantly) to send us to a secondary school which involved a journey by bus and train. I also remember being drilled on how to deal with strangers, how to make sure that one always carried enough money to deal with emergencies, and so on. This was not a regime of neglect. And it had strict boundaries about what time one was expected home and what had to be done in the event of a change of plans. But it was not primarily about control.

Nor was it a culture of blame. Cuts and bruises and damage to property were seen as natural consequences of the kinds of activities in which we were involved. The solution was in our own hands; if we did not like the heat we could stay out of the kitchen, or the football match, or the camp, or anywhere else that was dangerous. Ascribing blame implies that the system is under control, and that blame can be attached to the person or people who let things go wrong in the first place.

We have seen recently, and quite graphically, the way in which the blame culture has led to a narrowing of the range of opportunities for schoolchildren, as at least one major teachers' union in the UK has advised its members not to take children on school trips because of the risk that they will be sued if anything should go wrong. However, my purpose in exploring the notion of complexity in educational settings goes beyond the reporting of phenomena that have received a great deal of attention in the national press over the last year or so.

The rise in the blame culture has occurred at the same time as the rise in the accountability culture. It has also occurred at the same time as growing concern about bullying. If one looks at the notion of a complex system, with repeated patterns at different levels of organization, then the possibility of links between these elements, not causal links but nevertheless similarities in overall patterns, arises as a possible area for investigation.

This is not to say that systems of accountability are the same as bullying. However, creating a bureaucratic system with which participants can never fully comply puts a weapon into the hands of the bully, and a means by which they can undermine the position of others in their organization. If we go back 50 years, there were tests and examinations in schools, and there were end-of-year reports and school inspections, but they were never elevated to a principle according to which schools should be organized. There was also certainly bullying, normally in the form of initiation ceremonies into schools or clubs, but I do not remember it as either as systematic or as sustained as cases of bullying that one reads about today. The introduction of systems of control and compliance have brought in their wake an increase in accountability, bullying and blame. The three are not the same, but they are similar in their basic assumption that people can be controlled, and that when a system which involves people goes wrong it is appropriate to look for somebody to punish.

It is in this sense that 'great' and 'small' aspects of an organization are intimately connected in a complex system, that the notion of a 'whole-school policy' makes some kind of sense. This is a notion which, I have to confess, I otherwise find to be almost completely devoid of practical import. If a school is seen as a complex system, then we can no longer take it for granted that a policy adopted by the headteacher can be passed down the line to everybody in the school. On the contrary, the various layers of organization resemble each other in their forms, and to change the culture of the school requires action at many different levels. The adoption of a policy by the governors will do little for the pupils in the school (apart from generating a contempt for policies) unless it is matched by action that is reflected at all levels in the organization.

Schools as organizations and systems can be run either as complex systems with many feedback loops ensuring a loose coordination between the patterns of behaviour at different levels, or they can be run as command and control structures with rigid accountability and line management. The notion that in large and complex organizations patterns tend to repeat themselves at different levels suggests that they cannot easily be both. And at that point, one might well say that it was a matter of personal preference; there are authoritarian heads who prefer command and control, and there are liberal heads who prefer an atmosphere where a thousand flowers can bloom. However, as I started this chapter by observing, I am persuaded that the core activity of a school or college, the process of learning, is fundamentally and by its nature uncontrollable. A command-and-control school will eventually squeeze out the place for creative and chaotic activities, the most important of which is learning.

There is a difficulty here, of course. I am as keen as anybody that public resources should be wisely and effectively deployed, and that implies a level of accountability. And this, in turn, suggests that what I have ruled out as impossible in the previous paragraph, the coexistence of creativity and accountability in one organization, is highly desirable. Whether it can be achieved, and if so how, is a question that has yet to be addressed.

A further illustration of a model that might be derived from complexity theory may be useful. As a starting point in setting out a model of complex behaviour, consider a simple system which exhibits complex or chaotic behaviour. The model for chaotic behaviour is the pendulum system shown in Figure 3.2. The system consists of two simple pendula, the smaller suspended from the bob of the larger. When set in motion, the behaviour of the system is chaotic.

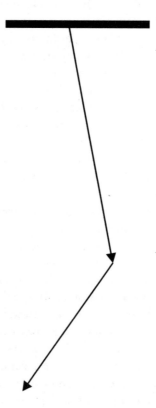

Figure 3.2   A complex system

In this context, 'chaotic' does not mean completely disorganized, nor even completely random; the pieces do not rush off over the other side of the room. It exhibits a kind of pattern of behaviour. Let us look at what complex behaviour is. In line with academic traditions, we can first analyse this system by breaking it down into its component parts. There is the top part, which is a simple pendulum, and it swings backward and forward with perfect regularity; you could set your watch by it. It follows the same pattern over and over again, and the bottom half of the system is another pendulum, which also swings backward and forward with perfect regularity. When you put those two simple systems together, what you get is a complex chaotic behaviour, which is not quite orderly and never quite repeats itself. It is fascinating to watch in the sense that all good executive toys are, because you never know quite what it is going to do next. It has the four characteristics found in complex systems: (1) a link to fractal geometry, such as that found in the Sierpinski Triangle; (2) recursive symmetries, or near-periodic motion; (3) sensitivity to initial conditions, or the butterfly effect; and (4) the presence of strange attractors. First of all, it has a behaviour which is linked to fractal geometry, and in this pattern there are infinite possible configurations that it can assume, and very finely divided disorder within the patterns – the top pendulum is moving regularly and then suddenly it is pulled back by the bottom pendulum. The second behaviour that complex systems illustrate is that there are what are called recursive symmetries: patterns at one level are not exactly the same but are similar to what is happening at a higher or lower level. The third pattern is sensitivity to initial conditions, or the butterfly effect. If I try to set the pendula swinging in exactly the same way as I did before, and if I am a fraction out, the pattern that the pendula follow will be slightly different from the pattern they followed the first time. And the fourth pattern of behaviour, the presence of strange attractors arises from dependence upon multiple feedback loops; the pendula are forever correcting the motion of each other by feedback communicated by tugs on the joining string.

To help me with the next step, I will need your imagination because I want the reader to imagine a visual aid that, for reasons that will become obvious, I cannot include in this book as a figure. Imagine one pendulum representing the rector or vice-chancellor of a university moving backwards and forwards, pulling the system in different directions. Just below the rector, imagine the academic board, each member moving backwards and forwards pulling in different directions. Suspended below the academic board are the deans, all on slightly different length pieces of string, all slightly different weights, sometimes all moving in the same direction, sometimes all pulling in opposite directions. Below the deans are the heads of departments, again all pulling backwards and forwards in different directions, and then the regular teachers in the departments down at the bottom, all moving to their own rhythm, which is slightly different. A colleague has suggested that I might not even stop there, but we might illustrate conflict within each person, representing individuals not as a single pendulum but as an arrangement of pendula pulling in different directions at different frequencies. Each individual would then be seen as a complex system of conflicting emotions being pulled in different directions, different objectives, different pressure groups persuading them to move.

I hope that image is clear, even if undrawable: different parts of the organization coordinated, loosely coordinated, but each influencing each other in mutual ways. Sometimes with fairly well-defined relationships, but not having the exact effect on the different levels above and below that you might have anticipated. What I hope that offers is a metaphor for the large organization, a large democratic organization or a large collegial organization like a university, which is different from our normal imagination. Our normal imagination of an organization in general is of a clockwork organization; in a clock there is one part of the mechanism that controls how fast it goes. We all have an idea of the organization where the rector or vice-chancellor says, 'These are going to be the goals of the institution', and that sets the framework for what happens in the institution. I am offering an alternative imagination of this complex organization, and this focuses attention on how we get decisions disseminated through the organization, how we make other parts of the organization aware of decisions that are made elsewhere. If our strategic objectives committee says, 'This institution promotes equal opportunities', how do we get that sold through the rest of the organization so that it actually happens? If our Quality Assurance Committee produces a Quality Assurance Handbook, how do we sell that to colleagues? This is an issue of internal marketing and one that we address too little. How do we sell those ideas to other parts of the institution?

The questions that arise in this context are important, and relate to the practical management of organizations that exhibit chaotic or complex behaviours. Unfortunately, the answers to those questions are not immediately obvious, and it will require much further research to fill out the understanding that we need to use complexity theory as a practical management tool. However, the vision that I have presented here does suggest some very interesting lines of exploration. All that we have at the moment is a relatively new model of an organization, and the intuitions that model incorporates.

It is in the nature of a model that it should embody a specialist language and implicit theories, about which events can be grouped together as 'the same', as I will argue in more detail in Chapter 4. In this sense, simply using complexity theory as a lens through which to view organizational behaviour suggests some ideas about what does and does not work in organizations. In general, we probably hold the opinion that organizations can be directed from the top, by edict and inspection, to a much greater extent than is true in practice. Complexity theory draws attention to the fact that lines of communication and accountability have to be made, not simply drawn upon an organizational chart. This in itself may be an important lesson that our politicians could learn.

Most of us probably work in organizations where the senior management think that they can control things from the centre by saying what has to be done. Those of us working in the organization go off in our own directions, being creative in our own small spheres, and somewhere between senior management and us the messages about mission and accountability get lost. Senior managers and politicians dream of the day when they could pass their messages on undistorted, undiluted, and the organization made more efficient. If only those working on the shop floor could be kept on task, how much more productive the organization would be.

In fact, the exact opposite is probably true. Improved systems of accountability and control would squeeze out unpredictability and creativity – the creativity that most of us need to get our job done in spite of the systems of accountability that are supposed to keep us focused on the job in hand. And this may be more true in schools and institutions of learning than it is anywhere else. A very important feature of complex organizations, as set out in the description here, is that there are recursive similarities; there are things that are similar at different levels within an organization. If you have an organization which promotes the development of individuals, that pattern will tend to be repeated at different levels. If you have an organization which is exploitative and controlling, those patterns will also tend to be repeated at different levels.

We do not know how to make sure that the organization picks up on beneficial cycles and how it gets out of negative cycles. What I am suggesting is that this is an area that needs to be given a great deal more attention in terms of study. I think that a good starting-point might be to use the metaphor of complex behaviour as a framework of analysis for looking at case-studies of particular organizations. For example, one might reanalyse historical cases that have been studied for other reasons.

One case study that has been reported extensively is that of Lucas Aerospace which had a rather interesting idea in the 1970s of disseminating its planning processes to the whole organization (Wainwright and Elliott 1982). Workers at all levels in the organization were going to be involved in planning what kind of products the company made, so that rather than senior management saying, 'We are a company that produces parts for aircraft', everyone in the company could be involved in saying, 'We might make some socially useful products as well: we might make electric vehicles, we might make heat-pumps, we might make hi-tech equipment for people with mobility difficulties.' What is interesting about that organization is that there were some very particular links between different levels, and there were levels of confidence and trust between those different levels which helped to make it possible for them to work and spread planning through the organization and make it successful. There were other things that made the experiment unsuccessful: one of those was that they had a senior management that said, 'We are an aircraft company. Why do we want to be doing all these other things? We should concentrate on the main business of making aircraft parts.'

There may be some very interesting lessons for educational institutions in such case-studies. The first striking point is that there is a strong tendency for managers in business to 'focus on the core activity of the organization'. This may work very well in business, in organizations that are low in complex behaviour and strong on accountability. But in education, it is less clear what the core business of a school is, and it is certain that parts of the educational process cannot be controlled in such precise ways. Conversely, as the case of Lucas Aerospace indicates, if we design our institutions to promote complex behaviours, nobody has precise control over where the organization will go. Complex organizations may find it difficult to summarize their mission in 50 words, or difficult to pursue their mission if they can.

All of which points to some serious difficulties which may arise if one tries to impose business models upon educational institutions. (It may also suggest there are possible difficulties in imposing business models on business organizations, but that would take me beyond the scope of my present concerns.) The question of which management structures can and cannot coexist within a single organization is one that needs much more detailed research.

From a purely 'management' perspective, the situation may be very much worse than I have suggested here; complexity theory is not a management tool in the way that such things are normally conceived. The butterfly effect implies that complex organizations (possibly all organizations to the extent that they exhibit complex behaviour) cannot be predicted and controlled in a mechanical way at all. The lessons of complexity theory are mostly negative, about what cannot be done.

On the other hand, perhaps the major issue management faces is to steer their organization towards or away from complex behaviour. We know that complex behaviour is more likely where there are multiple feedback loops and non-linear responses, and conversely that systems are more likely to behave in classical ways where there is little feedback and responses are linear. We may therefore be able to design organizations to behave in complex ways, or not, depending upon the structures that are put in place. Insights into how organizations should be designed in order to exhibit desired behaviours at all levels may be one of the valuable ways in which complexity theory could be used in the study of educational organizations. But a great deal more needs to be done in the course of that research to flesh out what are currently the bare bones of an intuition.

At the moment, we are left with some very tentative and anecdotal evidence. On one occasion I spent the night on an aircraft, flying across the Atlantic. And I was unfortunate because I was sitting next to a man who was rather large, and whose elbows stretched over the edge of the seat. Every two or three minutes, his elbow made contact with my ribs. The reason he was moving his elbows was because he was reading a book on management studies, on how to be an effective leader in management. Whenever he got to an interesting section, he took out his pen and highlighted it so that he could keep in mind what made an effective leader in management, and in the process he woke me up. It occurred to me then that I did not need to know any more; I knew exactly what kind of organization this person was going to be working in, and furthermore I was very glad I did not work in it. This is an issue of the style of management at one level which tends to get repeated and transmitted through to different levels, not automatically – there is nothing mechanical that says it has to be this way. But a person who is inconsiderate on a plane is likely to be an inconsiderate manager.

But this intuition, that the whole organization can be seen in a single unit and vice versa, if borne out by further research has very important implications for the governance of educational institutions. It would mean that an understanding of the learning process would need to be at the heart of every aspect of the organization, and that an organization that insisted upon treating its members as 'customers' could not be an educational institution.

Chapter 4

Modelling

The topic of the preceding three chapters has been modelling; constructing explicit and specific models from game theory and chaos (or complexity) theory, and holding them up as patterns for understanding and explaining naturalistic, everyday phenomena. But they have been about something more profound than simply creating models. They have been about creating models in a very self-conscious and sceptical way. The whole of this book focuses upon the idea of developing theory, but not of developing theory for its own sake. The purpose is to develop theory in order to build better models, so that a wider range of events can be researched, understood and eventually made subject to effective policy.

It may seem something of an aside, or perhaps an indulgence of the theorist, to dwell on the nature of using theory and models to develop an understanding. But precisely because modelling must be explicit, it is important to make some mention of the function of modelling here. The modelling must be explicit because otherwise the model can achieve too much significance. The model may assume the stature of a description of real life, or worse yet it may be understood as 'reality'. There is a difference between a model as a description of reality, and the model as a lens through which to view 'reality'. It is in that second sense of modelling, as providing a lens through which to view events while remaining sceptical as to whether there is anything that can be described as reality, that I intend to address in this chapter, and to use models in the rest of this book. As soon as that self-consciousness about the artificiality of models is lost, one runs the risk of reifying the concepts used, of falling into the belief that one has, at last, found the true account of what is going on, and ultimately of losing track of the purpose of theory in the first place.

I am not arguing that all models are equally good. I am certainly arguing that some models are better than others. But even if we can identify a better model, it is still the case that there may be many competing models that are equally good, and perhaps whole classes of models that are better still, but for which, for some reason, we have not yet recognized the need. But what needs to be recognized is that the alternative to explicit model-building is not avoiding the use of models; the alternative to explicit modelling is implicit modelling, which is modelling that is not reflective and is incapable of critical scrutiny.

Models are intimately tied to technical uses of language. An attempt to avoid the use of models, and implicitly to access 'reality' directly, generally also will make an appeal to 'common sense' and 'everyday language', the idea that models are an unnecessary complication that makes understanding more difficult.

For example, in his review of my book, *Theory of Education*, John Halliday (2005: 122) compares my arguments unfavourably with those of Richard Pring. He refers to Pring's preference for everyday language and notes, 'One problem with [my book] is that it seems to fall foul of Pring's requirement not to say something with technical language when ordinary language is perfectly adequate.' In many ways this is an attractive argument, that everyday language is more accessible, and if what is being put forward is relatively simple, there is no need to make it more difficult by clothing it in jargon.

This can be frustrating, because at one level I agree. Jargon and technical complications frequently give the appearance of having been used more as an obstacle to newcomers and an obfuscation than as an aid to critical enquiry. I also agree that when one comes to the end of a long and complicated technical explanation, one can often feel that the conclusion is straightforward, or simple, or obvious. And that raises the question of whether a diversion into technical language and methods was, indeed, worthwhile. So it seems to me appropriate to add a diversion here in defence, if not exactly in praise, of jargon.

In the eleventh and twelfth centuries, stonemasons had a rule of thumb that stated that the load in a column or wall should be kept within the middle third of the structure. In order to achieve this result in the design of Gothic cathedrals, buttresses were deployed (the walls were thickened in such a way that the load remained within the middle third), pinnacles were added to the walls above roof-level (the downward load was increased to keep the load within the middle third of the wall), and eventually flying buttresses were designed (creating a virtual thickening of the walls while maintaining the light and airy structure). But all of these tactics were used to good effect by medieval stonemasons.

Many centuries later, when I was an engineering student, I was able to use the developments in mathematics, most notably the calculus developed by Newton, to analyse forces within structures, and the conditions under which the material of a stone or concrete wall would be put into tension rather than compression. Since stone and concrete are strong in compression but weak in tension, this condition was assumed to be one of collapse. And with those not inconsiderable mathematical tools at our disposal, what we were able to show was that in order to ensure that a wall or column can remain intact, the load must be kept within the middle third.

Should we conclude that the technicality, the jargon (for there certainly is a jargon of calculus), the complication of the modern methods were pointless if all that they did was confirm a result that the medievals had assumed? I certainly want to conclude that that was not the case, and that in this instance the use of technical language was justified. The calculus enabled this situation to be analysed but also brought within the purview of the engineer other structures of steel and other materials that could be made subject to similar analyses. More important than the specific result was the approach which allowed for such analysis, the development of strict methods of modelling and of describing physical configurations. The methods were not always used successfully, and were frequently found to be tragically wanting when a new phenomenon which had not previously been incorporated into the model was encountered. Such was the case for brittle fracture, metal fatigue and the buckling of welded box-girders. But the modelling which had been developed for the simple cases was eventually adapted to the more complex.

The use of technical descriptions can, therefore, help in the development of theory. The word jargon itself tends to be applied to the use of technical language where it is neither useful nor appropriate (especially for communication to a lay audience). Consequently, one person's technical language tends to be another's jargon. But at its best, jargon represents a way of

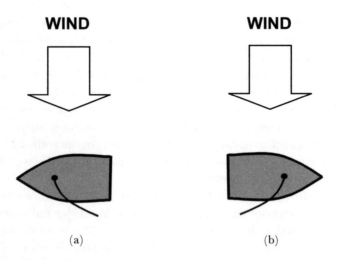

(a)   (b)

Figure 4.1   Sailing dinghy on (a) a starboard reach or (b) a port reach

describing events which cannot easily be described in everyday language. Jargon then stands in relation to everyday language as an alternative paradigm, an incommensurable framework of analysis. An example may help to illustrate this (see Figure 4.1).

When a novice first learns to sail, he or she learns that when the boat is sailing with the wind from one side, it is said to be on a reach. If we imagine the wing blowing down the direction of the page, the boat may be on a reach going either to the left or the right, a starboard reach or a port reach respectively.

In order to get from position (a) to position (b) the dinghy needs to turn through 180. This could be done by turning the bow of the dinghy first towards the wind, and then continuing to turn in the same direction (clockwise in the diagram). Similarly, to move from position (b) to position (a) the dinghy could be pointed into the wind, and then continue further to arrive at position (a) (an anti-clockwise motion in the diagram).

The sailor describes both of these manoeuvres with the same word; the dinghy 'tacks' from one reach to the other, or 'goes about'. Lovers of plain language and haters of jargon, especially if they have been raised on the technology of the motor car, will resist this technical language and suggest that we call these two manoeuvres 'turning right' and 'turning left' respectively.

Alternatively, the sailor in the dinghy might choose to get from position (a) to position (b) by pointing the boat away from the wind and continuing on to make a 180 turn (in an anti-clockwise direction in the diagram). For those who prefer plain language, the boat could 'turn left' to get from position (a) to position (b). The sailor uses a different term: the dinghy 'gybes'. A gybe happens when the stern of the boat passes through the wind, and the sailor would of course describe a boat in position (b) that 'turned right' as performing a gybe.

The dinghy sailor therefore groups two of the possible manoeuvres together as 'tacks' and two as 'gybes'. The lover of plain language groups one of the tacks and one of the gybes together as 'turning left', and the other of each as 'turning right'. Before proceeding further with the question of whether the jargon is right or wrong, this very clear difference needs remarking; the two different ways of describing what the dinghy does form different groupings. Events which are brought together as similar in one form of expression are singled out as distinctive in the other. The language that is being used makes certain comparisons appear obvious, while others are made more difficult.

For the sailor, the direction of the wind is all-important, and the reason for grouping tacks with tacks and gybes with gybes is that different issues arise in the different contexts. For example, the risks associated with gybing, particularly the risk of capsize, are very different from those of tacking. As a consequence, the routines for each, the things that a dinghy sailor needs to be watching out for, are very different. It may be some time before the novice sailor learns all of this, however, as gybing is considered to be difficult to control, and lessons in how to do it normally come after a good deal of experience has been gained.

Of course, a technical language or jargon is relative to the situations one is trying to use and to describe. The motorist, to whom the direction of the wind will rarely be of much significance, will continue to describe their man-oeuvres as turning left or turning right. In the UK, right-turns have more in common with all other right-turns than they do with left-turns, since they normally involve crossing the oncoming line of traffic. On the other hand, if we wished to describe driving in terms which took into account national differences in driving regulations, we might need to develop a different jargon, and start talking about turning to the off-side, or turning to the near-side, for example.

Technical language or jargon, therefore, can be seen to perform a useful function. The word 'jargon' is generally reserved to describe technical lan-guage which one does not understand or think necessary. But taking it at its most positive, technical language may permit the straightforward descrip-tion of situations which would be difficult to translate into everyday lan-guage. Technical language may also facilitate the grouping of events which are of particular concern or interest within a particular technology. Such technical language is prevalent in many areas of special interest, especially where the area demands specialized skills. The baseball specialist will be very familiar with the fast ball, the change-up, the slider, the curveball and the knuckleball. The corresponding aficionado of cricket may talk about bowling over the wicket, inswingers and leg-breaks. Who knows what it all means? It takes years of study to understand the intricacies, and then a single word can convey a range of meanings and implications.

Of course, this leads on to the consideration of the least attractive aspect of jargon, namely the fact that it can be used to exclude 'outsiders' from con-versation about the technical area of expertise, and not necessarily by mal-icious intent. I once bought a book on a technical subject that I wanted to know about (Osborne 1976), only to discover after several days' hard work, that I had not adequately understood the technical language in the title (8080 Programming for Logic Design) when I selected it. I suppose that the author had assumed that anybody who would be interested in the con-tent of the book would be familiar enough with the jargon to understand the exact nuance of the title. However, jargon has a bad name when it is used to exclude participants even though there is no substantive obstacle to their understanding. This feature of jargon has given rise to a series of books with titles beginning, *How to Bluff Your Way in* ... But as has been noted above, jargon and technical language can serve a useful function in enabling the convenient regrouping of phenomena which would be very difficult to describe in everyday language.

In this positive sense, jargon and technical language may be seen as connected with paradigm shifts. A technical language, such as that used by sailors, offers a parallel description of events that *could* be described without recourse to jargon; the test of the value of the special turns of phrase is the economy of language among the group that understands it, and the ability to bring together novel or useful comparisons on the basis of groupings that would not readily be available in everyday language. Usefulness and convenience, rather than truth or correctness, become the acid test.

However, along with paradigm shifts, jargon may be very difficult, or even impossible, to step outside of and gain a clear external view. To the seasoned sailor, there may be no connection between two events that the landlubber would happily class together as 'turning right'. The two events would simply not be in the same category, so anything that the events actually did have in common would be likely to be overlooked by the sailor. Similarly, two events which the sailor happily grouped together would simply not be comparable for the landlubber. Technical language has all the properties of being incommensurable with other technical descriptions, and of hiding certain comparisons while making others stand out.

This is not an absolute restriction, in the sense that things that are easily described in a jargon may be difficult, but not impossible, to describe in another. We can imagine a sailor giving warning to his or her crew by saying, 'We are going to take a right-turn, but not one of those right-turns where the sail comes from one side of the boat to the other slowly and in a controlled way, but one of those right-hand turns where the wind gets behind the sail and whips it across to the other side of the boat swiftly and rather violently. Be careful not to be hit on the head by the boom.' But equally, we can imagine that it will not be long before the sailor comes to realize the value of the standard form of words: 'Ready to gybe!'

So without wishing to become deterministic in the notion that the nature of the vocabulary and concepts employed shapes the discourse precisely, and the discourse determines what can and cannot be said, nevertheless we can see that the use of a specific technical language does increase the likelihood of making some specific comparisons and coming to some specific conclusions. But if that is true for a jargon or a technical language, it must also be true of everyday language. The form of the language makes it easier to pursue some lines of argument than others.

The argument that a specialist language carries with it a predisposition towards certain models and theories has been further developed in discourse analysis to argue that the nature of the discourse, the commonly employed concepts and references, shape what can and cannot be said by participants in the discourse. And, it hardly needs saying, everyday language also contains structural assumptions about what can be described easily and what comparisons are most obvious. It is worth considering what is implied by the most obvious elements in everyday discourse. Kipling said that he kept six honest serving men and that they taught him all he knew; and, as he indicates in the poem, the one which probably taught him most, especially as a child, was 'Why?' 'Why?' is such a powerful question, and so easy to ask, yet what does it imply about the nature of a suitable response?

Why do boys underperform in the education system? Why are men more prone to dyslexia than women? Why are there not more working-class students at ancient universities? Such questions invite the identification of a cause, something that differentiates between the two groups concerned (men and women in the first two questions, social classes in the third) that could account for the different outcomes. Our everyday language and common sense are suffused by assumptions of single-centredness which make it much easier to ask this kind of question than any other.

It is perhaps worth noting at this point that the term 'cause' has suffered a fairly radical circumscription of meaning in the last 300 years. Aristotle identified four separate kinds of cause: formal cause, final cause, material cause and efficient cause. If one was to ask the cause of a particular statue being just as it was, rather than any other way, there might be four answers. The formal cause for it being this way is that it is a statue that represents a horse, and therefore the statue shares something with horses that it does not share with people. The final cause for it being this way was the purpose of the sculptor: he or she intended this statue to stand in a particular place when complete. The material cause for it being this way rather than any other is that it is made of marble, rather than bronze or wood, and therefore has particular properties. And finally the efficient cause for it being this way are the individual blows with a hammer and chisel that the sculptor has administered, and whose imprint may be seen in the final statue.

Since the advancement of science in the seventeenth century we have moved a long way, and normally expect to be given an efficient cause when we ask, 'Why?' Occasionally, when we ask somebody why they acted in a particular way, we may be expecting a final cause, or purpose, to be expressed. But even here, in the explanation of human agency, efficient causes are increasingly resorted to.

In Chapter 9, in the context of Vygotsky's work, I look at his notion that psychology has restricted itself to a single type of explanation, namely stimulus-response. I would say that this is a specific example of a broader trend towards a focus upon efficient causes. We seek a single (normally genetic or social) factor that can explain educational phenomena. This narrowing focus is increasingly wrapped up in the common-sense and everyday question, 'Why?', and responses beginning, 'Because . . .'

Questions which are multicentred are much harder to ask. What function does it serve for a group of people to divide themselves between the options available in the proportions that we observe? This is relatively easily translated into the question, Why do more of a particular group do X rather than Y? And from there it is only a small step to, Why do boys underperform in the education system? But one can see that this final formulation is not the same as the initial question, because a back-translation is unlikely to work. The final statement is much more likely to be back-translated as, 'What is the cause of boys' underachievement in the education system?'

In translating a technical language into everyday language, something may be lost. It may appear that what is being said is trivial in everyday language, and that may, in part, be because the active possibilities of the technical perspective have been ignored for the sake of clarity. But, nevertheless, the everyday translation is not the exact equivalent of the technical phrasing.

And ultimately, that is why there is a need from time to time to divert into technical formulations. I think that the radical possibilities of game-theoretical and linear programming models can, to some extent, be captured in the everyday notion that there are more ways than one to achieve a result, or there is more than one right way of doing anything. But that does not mean that such a statement in everyday language captures all of the possibilities offered by a complex technical model, or, possibly more importantly, that the common-sense assumptions are so forcibly interrogated in the light of the everyday language formulation. Technical expressions are sometimes needed simply because they are technical expressions, and they have the capacity to make the familiar strange.

Up to this point, I have been arguing that technical language, or indeed jargon, can be useful in expressing the main features of models in succinct ways. However, if that case is granted, there remains the complementary danger of modelling, that the description of a model might be confused with a claim to describe 'reality'.

There is a very important issue here, namely that there is generally confusion between an understanding of behaviour 'as if it were ...' and an understanding of behaviour 'because it is ...' The economist argues, more or less as a matter of professional identity, that we can understand a great deal about the way people behave if we think about what they would do *if they were to act in such a way* as to maximize their utility. This is an explicit model, and the claim is that if we hold rational, utility-maximization up to phenomena, and use it as a lens through which to describe events, we can account for a great deal of what we see in those terms. But this is very different from claiming that people usually act to maximize their utility, that they always act to maximize their utility, or that it is part of human nature that people should act to maximize their utility, which are progressively more mistaken ways of interpreting the application of a model.

There is a tendency to reify intellectual concepts and move from 'This is a useful intellectual construct' to 'This is what happens, or should happen.' For example, the idea that individuals act to maximize their utility is an interesting concept, and may help to describe how some people act, even if they do not act strictly in accordance with the principle. There is a simple step, frequently but erroneously made by policy-makers, that consequently we should distribute opportunities through a market mechanism, or a pseudo-market mechanism. For this reason, it is important to be very clear and explicit about what is and what is not involved in the process of formal modelling.

In the course of this book I have advanced a number of models developed from game theory and chaos (or complexity) theory. I have chosen these particular models because they seem to me to have a number of features that are desirable. They are non-deterministic, and so they allow some space within which individuals can be expected to exercise free will without contradicting the models. And they allow for the fact that the links between individual behaviour and group behaviour are complex, and not the outcome of a simple arithmetic. In this way they make room for emergent properties of groups that cannot be accounted for entirely in terms of the individuals who make up the group. For all of these reasons I would maintain that the models that I am advancing here are better than single-centred models that seek causes, or factors, that explain particular outcomes.

I am also arguing that when we hold these models up against some anecdotal experience, and even some research findings, it would appear that the models have some explanatory power.

But beyond that, I am certainly not arguing that game-theory models or chaos-theory models are the only multicentred models that might be useful. I may be lazy enough to stick with those that I have found, or lack imagination to formulate other equally good models, or simply think that I already have enough to do researching the models that I have already identified, but I am not making any kind of claim to have identified 'reality' or even to have identified the ultimate models of educational behaviour.

I am not even claiming that the specific formulation of the game-theory models I have advanced here is necessarily correct. Indeed, in the following chapters I will draw attention to areas where it is unclear exactly how the model should be developed or applied. The result is a programme of research designed to improve on the models that are set out in this book.

I suppose that in this sense I am making the equivalent of Newton's famous claim that '*Hypothesis non fingo*' ('I do not make hypotheses'). In Newton's case I think that there is reason to believe that his sentence should perhaps have been completed, 'I do not make hypotheses, because I am telling you the truth about reality, and how objects behave.' But at least in my own case I can be sure that I do not make hypotheses in the sense of arguing that people are playing a two-person game against Nature, or that a classroom is a multiperson non-zero-sum game. What I am inviting the reader of this book to do is to look at career choices *as though they were* two-person games against Nature, or to examine a classroom setting *as though it were* a multiperson non-zero-sum game. Does that highlight any interesting aspects of phenomena that we observe, which were mysterious before or overlooked? Does it suggest any interesting lines of research? Does it suggest some fruitful lines for policy?

By the end of this book I hope that such a concise statement as 'Career choices can be understood as a two-person game against Nature', will appear as straightforward, and as pregnant with overtones and suggestions as the phrase 'Ready to gybe' is to a sailor. To those who still prefer an ordinary-language explanation of what this means, that is the purpose of this book. But in the end, I believe that there is a place for technical language or jargon in educational studies. We do not hesitate when describing assessments to use such terms as formative and summative, or norm-referenced and criterion-referenced, even though it is possible to render these terms into ordinary language. This technical language refers to distinctions that every educationist ought to be able to draw, and which can be assumed in any discussion about assessment. I simply propose the inclusion of a little more technical language, including the terms single-centred and multicentred, to describe theory and policy.

Part 2

Practice

Chapter 5

Classroom Management

Introduction

It may sound strange, when I have emphasized 'policy' so strongly, to begin with an issue that many would hardly categorize as policy at all. However, classroom management concerns policy at the microlevel, with teachers setting standards of behaviour, classroom rules, patterns of interaction, and so on, which all set the policy framework within which pupil behaviour takes place. I therefore propose to take it as my first illustration of policy, to explore the possibility of policy-based research.

There is a further reason for choosing classroom management as a starting point. In the preceding chapter I stressed that multicentred approaches to educational research would require us to imagine a homogeneous group of pupils, placed in a similar setting, but yet behaving in different ways. Rather than looking for the individual characteristics that make one pupil pay attention and another play battleships with a friend, we should be looking at overall classroom management features that ensure that only two pupils play battleships, rather than 20. In a multicentred approach, there is no need to seek out causes for conscientiousness or unruliness; what is of interest is how the class divides itself between the two (or more) attitudes.

I have placed considerable emphasis upon the idea that education research should examine the behaviour of groups rather than individuals, and that research models should be able to take into account the ways in which the behaviour of some members of the group may have repercussions on other members of the group. At its very simplest, every teacher will watch those pupils who head for the back row of the classroom as the pupils enter the classroom. But physical arrangements and logic dictate that only a limited proportion of the class can sit in the back row. If the seats are all occupied, the next child, whatever their attitude, must sit elsewhere. In the classroom, the key features of multicentred approaches can be seen where the actions of each member of the group have an instant and sometimes powerful effect on the choices of others, and the possibility that behaviours can be amplified or attenuated.

One of the earliest surprises that faces a teacher is that the atmosphere of classes can vary so much from year to year. Working in a large comprehensive school, each year-group may involve 300 pupils. The 'law of averages' suggests to the untutored mind that 300 young people picked out of a population at random will be much like another 300. But teachers know that this 300 have been together through most of their schooling. They have developed an *esprit de corps*, for better or worse, and have worked off each other to produce the overall result that every teacher encounters when they enter a classroom. The result is that some year-groups are thoroughly hard work, while others are a delight to be with. Groups develop their own dynamic, their own character, quite apart from the individuals who make them up.

In spite of this, 'classroom management', as it appears in the research literature, rarely deals with groups of pupils. Classroom management and behaviour management are conceived in terms of a series of one-off interactions between the teacher and a pupil. The teacher is to provide a system of rewards and punishments (or stimuli) for the pupil, as a result of which the pupil's behaviour (response) can be steered in the direction the teacher wishes. It is of great importance in this scheme of things (a scheme of things which is markedly behaviouristic) that the teacher's behaviour should be completely consistent, which is to say not influenced by the immediate circumstances, the interventions of other people, her mood, or anything else. Classroom management, therefore, as it appears in the literature, is either about the logistics of managing the materials necessary for teaching in the classroom, or it is about dyadic relationships between a teacher and a pupil, all interactions being assumed to take place in a social vacuum. It specifically is not about managing the social interactions of a dynamic group of people.

This mismatch between the teacher's task, of living with and influencing the development of 30 social beings, and the framework of educational research, which deals only with a one-to-many relationship between a teacher and 30 isolated individuals, serves to throw up many of the issues that are involved in developing multicentred approaches to educational research and replacing single-centred models of research. Although similar issues will recur throughout the discussion of the various examples in this book, there is hardly anywhere where the need for multicentred imagination is greater than in the classroom.

I have not entirely left behind the notion of the lone teacher dealing with 30, isolated individuals. I will return to it again as a special case of the framework that I am setting out here. But before I come to that, let me set out the framework that I intend to use for describing, and researching, classroom management.

The classroom model

As with many of the topics that I am examining, I am trying to pose questions which will test current models for understanding classroom management. I also wish to suggest new models which articulate aspects that cannot be accommodated in the standard approaches. The result is a model which is more complicated than those that are usually used to manage behaviour, and which overcomes some of the simple dichotomies of traditional models. The model that I am putting forward remains a simplification and an abstraction from reality. However, what I am suggesting is that the new models offer opportunities for developing experimental approaches which are more satisfying and more useful in the long-run that excessively simplified models.

One of the difficulties I face is that the shortcomings of traditional models are not always easily apparent but are highlighted by features of the new models. I therefore propose to set out an approach to structuring an understanding of classroom management based on multiperson game theory. When I have set out that model I will return again to the critique that it provides for more traditional models.

Let me suppose first of all, by way of abstraction, that in a class of 30 pupils each pupil faces a decision whether to cooperate or defect. That is to say they can cooperate by sitting still, studying quietly and not arguing with the teacher, or they can defect by questioning the statements made by the teacher, demanding further amplification of the explanations or by engaging in even more disruptive behaviour.

As an aside, it might be worth mentioning that the terminology of cooperation and defection comes directly from the famous 'prisoner's dilemma' where two prisoners are arrested by the police and put in separate cells and persuaded that they should confess to a crime and implicate their friend so as to avoid the punishment which they will receive if they refuse to confess while their friend confesses. However, in the context of classroom management I do not wish to suggest that cooperation or defection carry any moral overtones. Sitting silently in the class and not being excessively demanding may be perfectly appropriate in a class of 30 in a secondary school, while posing difficult questions and asking for extended explanations may be equally appropriate in a university seminar. But I continue in the use of cooperation and defection as these have come into the discourse of multiperson game theory as separate labels for two distinct courses of action.

Let me further suppose not only that each pupil has to make the choice between two courses of action, which for the sake of convenience are labelled cooperating and defecting, but that each pupil derives some benefit which depends upon the total decisions made by each individual in the class. And let me suppose that the benefit, however it is defined, whether in terms of satisfaction felt by the pupil, the amount of time the teacher devotes to each pupil, or some other indicator, can be unambiguously measured. This last assumption is, of course, not without its difficulty, and I will return to the practical implementation of such models at the end of this chapter.

Consider the situation set out in Figure 5.1 (unruly classroom). The left hand of this graph is labelled zero on the x axis. At this extreme left-hand edge, no pupils are choosing to defect. The line CC indicates the benefits available to pupils who cooperate, while the line DD indicates the benefits available to pupils who defect. At the extreme left-hand edge of the figure, where all pupils are cooperating, a larger benefit is available to the pupil who chooses to defect.

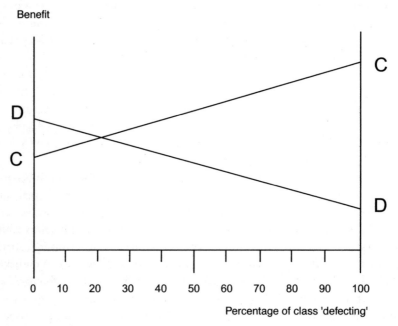

Figure 5.1   Unruly classroom

The physical, if somewhat simplified, meaning of this can be relatively easily grasped. In a class that is well-behaved, a child who asks awkward questions and behaves in an undisciplined way can reap considerable benefits in terms of increased teacher attention and kudos from fellow pupils. It is a case where the squeaky wheel gets the grease.

As we move progressively towards the right-hand edge of the graph, towards the position where 100 per cent of the class is defecting, the reward for those cooperating increases while the reward for those defecting decreases. The two lines indicating the benefits to the pupils cross when approximately 22 per cent of the class are defecting.

Again, the physical meaning of this can be relatively easily understood; when 20 per cent of the class is misbehaving, whatever teacher attention is available, or whatever kudos is to be achieved by being the class barrack-room lawyer or class clown, has to be spread rather thinly over many people. At the same time, the teacher is likely to be rather more appreciative of those who are not making his or her life more difficult.

Now imagine that I come into the classroom when all the pupils are seated patiently at their desks waiting for the lesson to start. At that moment all pupils are receiving the benefit C and there is therefore an incentive for one child to defect. I might imagine, for example, one child shouting out a comment to attract the attention of his or her peers. The class as a whole now is in a position where one child (or roughly 3 per cent of the class) is defecting, and as a consequence the class moves to the right along the graph. At this point there remains an increased benefit for the second child to defect, perhaps answering the call of the first child. The second child starts talking to the first. The class now has 6 per cent of the pupils defecting and the class moves further to the right. The class continues to move to the right as more and more children defect until roughly 22 per cent of the class is defecting, at which point there is no further additional benefit for more children to defect and the classroom reaches an equilibrium.

The same equilibrium might have been approached from the opposite side. Imagine instead of arriving at a class of patient well-behaved children I had arrived at a classroom to find a riot, with 100 per cent of the children defecting. At that point there is a greatly increased benefit available to the first child who behaves by moving from the defecting line to the cooperating line. The first child cooperates and the class moves slightly to the left. There remains a highly advantageous benefit from cooperating over defecting. We would expect the second, third and fourth child to start to cooperate. The class moves progressively to the left until there is no further benefit to be gained from cooperating and the class again arrives at the equilibrium with roughly 22 per cent cooperating and roughly 78 per cent defecting.

One might well reflect upon a number of classrooms that one has seen where a small group of unruly children, normally those who have found their way into the back row of the classroom, are chatting, playing games, distracting each other or in some other way misbehaving, while the majority of the class continues with their work under the watchful eye of the teacher.

If we now move on to consider Figure 5.2 (Revolution in the classroom), it will be noted that the overall appearance of the figure is very similar to that of the unruly classroom. However, there is an important difference between the two figures, which is that the benefits for cooperating and defecting have been completely interchanged. The resulting difference in classroom management is dramatic. In this case if I come into the classroom when all the children are seated at their desks there is a substantial benefit for each child to be gained by cooperating. The classroom will therefore remain stable with all children continuing in their obedient and cooperative behaviour. On the other hand, if I come into the classroom when it is in a state of riot there is a substantial increased benefit to be gained by the children who defect and no incentive for them to start cooperating. The classroom therefore remains with 100 per cent of the participants rioting. As can be seen

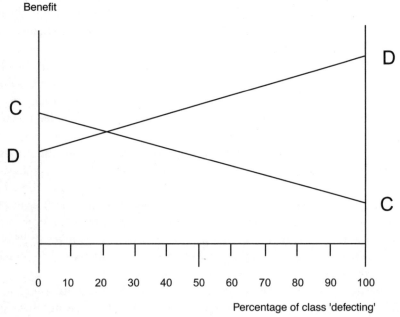

Figure 5.2   Revolution in the classroom

by taking the classroom in any intermediate position, if there are less than 22 per cent of the classroom defecting then the classroom tends to move to a stable position at the left-hand edge of the graph, while if there are more than 22 per cent of the children defecting the class tends to move towards riot and the right-hand edge of the graph.

I have called this the recipe for a revolution because in normal circumstances, and as normally observed, the class will be perfectly well-behaved. However, should the critical mass of children start to misbehave, or refuse the authority of the teacher, the situation degenerates to become dramatically out of hand. One remembers stories of demagogues who have established a firm and iron rule only to have it disrupted when a few pupils, or possibly even one pupil, stand up to them. It is only in this extraordinary situation when the class has crossed this rubicon that one can see the full structure of the classroom management system. However, I would suggest that we have all seen colleagues who have perfectly orderly classrooms but where there is a frisson of resentment or danger bubbling below the surface which suggests that they are teaching in a revolutionary classroom.

In Figure 5.3 ('Perfect' classroom), I have put the reward structure which is normally considered to be that of a classroom that is being well managed by a professional teacher in perfect conditions. When I was being trained as

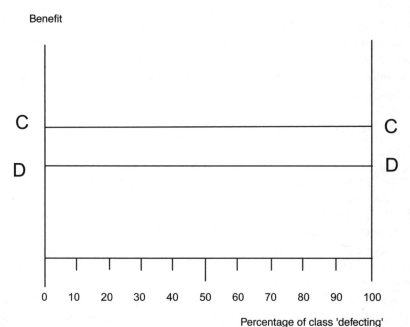

Figure 5.3   'Perfect' classroom

a teacher it was suggested that this was the kind of reward structure that I should set up in the classroom, where each individual child can expect the same premium of benefit for cooperating over defecting and where the decision of each child is completely independent of all the others. No matter how many children choose to defect, it will always be to the advantage of each individual to cooperate. The result is that this classroom moves progressively to the left and is stable, with none of the children defecting and no child having any incentive to defect.

Such an arrangement is certainly the counsel of perfection as far as teachers are concerned, as it requires absolute patience and consistency in order to produce a reward structure even approximating this model. A number of other features may be noted. In particular, this is the model of traditional classroom management. The decisions of individual pupils are not linked and there is no situational change in the benefit for cooperating or defecting. Children who defect are assumed to be mistaken and can be brought back into cooperation by the appropriate administration of rewards and punishments. In such models it is assumed that what the pupils learn will largely be determined by the style that the teacher adopts or by some other characteristics in the individual child's background.

The perfect classroom represented in Figure 5.3 is a static analysis of classroom management. Each individual responds to a reward structure that has been set up and established by the teacher, but there is no interaction between the behaviour of other pupils and the benefits that are available. In contrast with this, the combination of the patterns of the organization of classrooms set out in the three figures (and by a range of other combinations of benefits for cooperation or defection) can be seen as constituting a dynamic model of classroom management.

Anecdotal evidence

I have thought about this a good deal since I stopped being a classroom teacher, although I must say I was not quite so detached in my reflections when I actually had to be in a classroom in front of 30 children. I have come to the conclusion that, unwittingly, I tended to structure the rewards and benefits in my classroom in the manner set out approximately in Figure 5.4. This arrangement is very similar, in effect, to the unruly classroom. Although the benefits for cooperation remain constant the benefits for defecting decrease dramatically, that is to say the first child who defected received considerably more of my attention as a result of their defection, but as increasing numbers defected, that attention, being shared among many, decreased in proportion

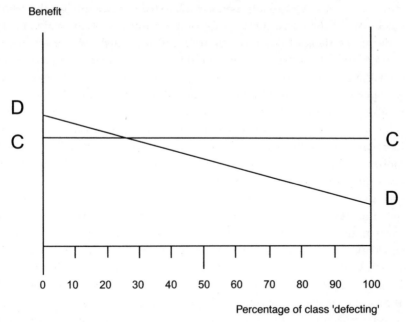

Figure 5.4 My classroom

to the number defecting. The result was that in any class of 30, I could expect to have four or five pupils, usually boys, sitting in the back row creating a nuisance, or in some other way demonstrating that they were defecting. The obvious delight which they got from winding up their teacher was probably benefit enough to explain why they chose this course of action.

There is one further important point that needs to be emphasized here. Having set up my system of classroom rewards and punishments as shown in Figure 5.4, and having achieved the result of having four or five unruly children defecting, it remains the case that the model does not imply that the behaviour of any individual child is determined. Each child who defects may still be seen as fully responsible for their own actions and therefore culpable for their own misbehaviour. At the time I found this very frustrating. Having suffered an hour with a class with four unruly boys, I would take one of them on one side, who I presumed to be the ringleader. I would explain to him that a clever chap like him could derive great benefit from studying the material in my class, and that he ought to pay more attention and work harder. Generally speaking, in terms of individual behaviour this had the desired effect, and the next lesson he would turn up determined that he was going to concentrate and apply himself to his studies on this occasion. But my effort was to no avail because some other individual readily stepped into the breach that he had left, and I still had four or five unruly children in the back row of the classroom. In fact, I generally had four or five unruly children at the back of the class, though not necessarily the same ones on every occasion. This separation of the individual behaviour from the overall group behaviour is important in leaving room for personal pride in achievement or personal responsibility, or lack of it. It is at the heart of what I mean by 'multicentredness'.

I said earlier that I did not wish to attach moral overtones to the terms 'cooperating' and 'defecting', although I may appear to have done so up to this point. Although I have described classrooms in terms of behaving and misbehaving, and aligned that with cooperation and defection, there is no necessary reason to suppose there is a moral overtone to the behaviours concerned. The decision whether a country should drive on the left-hand side or the right-hand side of the road might be modelled in Figure 5.2 as a revolutionary situation. The only two outcomes which are stable are that everybody should drive on the left-hand side of the road or everybody should drive on the right-hand side of the road. The lack of benefit arising from a small group of people choosing to drive on the unconventional side are so great as to provide the incentive to move back towards conformity either on the left or on the right. There is no moral difference between driving on the left-hand side of the road or the right-hand side of the road, simply a difference.

Similarly, from the point of view of classroom management, there is only a model that covers two course of action. The teacher may prefer one of them over the other but from a theoretical point of view there is nothing to say that cooperation is necessarily to be preferred over defection. We might contrast those settings that I have described above with the situation in a seminar or discussion group. Here the tutor may be trying to develop a revolutionary setting. He or she comes into the seminar room and conversation stops. The object of the exercise is then to get enough individuals questioning, seeking amplification and putting forward their points of view so that the discussion takes off and moves into a heated debate, where all those present take an active part. We might contrast this with the 'unruly classroom' setting, where a lively discussion is taken up by a small group of those present, but the majority look on but do not contribute. And this might also be distinguished from the 'perfect classroom' setting, where students make comments addressed to the tutor, and seek the tutor's approval and affirmation, but the sense of discussion between the students never really becomes established.

What I hope this illustrates is that constructing models of classroom management as multiperson games can offer an interesting and dynamic insight into different styles of classroom organization. In a qualitative sense, it seems to me to illuminate some aspects of my experience, and provides a way for me to reflect upon my own teaching performance, and to structure the way that I view my own interactions with students.

However, to go beyond that anecdotal level of understanding, it will be necessary to go back to the two assumptions made at the beginning of this process of modelling, and to examine whether they are justified, and perhaps more importantly whether there is any course of research which could support and underpin them.

I started the modelling process with two assumptions in order to make the model possible. In the first place I assumed that each pupil in the class had to choose between only two courses of action. They could choose either to cooperate or to defect. It may be argued that in any real classroom pupils face a much wider range of choices. They may choose to be enthusiastic about the topic and invest energy and additional personal research in activities, or they may choose simply to complete the task set and comply with the instructions of the teacher. They may choose to read a comic under the desk, gaze out of the window, throw paper aeroplanes or be abusive and violent. In short, there are many ways in which they may choose to defect, and as many ways in which they may choose to cooperate. All of this is certainly true, yet for modelling purposes I suspect that the fiction that the pupils face a choice of only two courses of action must remain, however unpalatable the simplification that it represents.

In most cases, if one attempts to draw three lines on one of the figures, one comes to one of two conclusions: either only two of the lines contribute to the overall maximum benefit which the pupil can seek, or possibly one may draw three lines so that each contributes a part to the maximum benefit. That is to say, the system of classroom rewards and punishments may be such that some choices never make sense: gazing out of the window does not bring as much teacher approval as studying the work set, and neither does it command the respect of peers. In those circumstances, gazing out of the window is a choice, but it is always less attractive than one of the other options. Alternatively, the other choices may only become relevant in very special circumstances. The pupil who only has to choose between reading quietly and chatting with a neighbour quietly in an orderly classroom may be forced to choose between hiding under a desk and setting off the fire alarm when the classroom is in full riot.

But in either case, the equilibrium positions of the overall classroom configurations are such that only two of the lines actually contribute to the behaviour of the class as a whole at any one time. This is analogous to the result in two-person zero-sum games, that a pure strategy, or a mixed strategy of two pure strategies, will always dominate. The overall conclusion must therefore be that the present model implies that a choice between only two courses of action will dominate the overall pattern of classroom behaviour. In the end, of course, this is a question that can be tested through further empirical studies, whether in fact classroom organization and management can be understood in terms of a simple dichotomous choice in each case. For the moment I am suggesting that the model provides some advantages over existing models and offers a way of entering some empirical examinations of classroom management.

The other assumption that I made as a basis for developing the model of classroom management was that the level of benefit to be derived from any course of action could be easily identified and measured, whether that was in terms of the level of satisfaction as a pupil, the level of future reward for knowledge attained, or some other measure of classroom behaviour such as attention from the teacher or gold stars. That question of measuring benefit, and indeed the question of whether every member of a class of pupils can be characterized as having the same benefits or valuing the same outcomes, is extremely problematic. It is this aspect that should probably be the focus of future empirical studies.

It is a practical and empirical question whether benefit can be operationalized and if so, how. Pupils may derive benefit from 'cooperating' with the teacher in terms of marks awarded for work, the time and attention of the teacher or some other indicator. Using one of these methods of operationalization would allow studies to be conducted along the lines proposed here, and this would in turn inform subsequent, and better, modelling of classroom management. Even quite crude measures of 'benefit' would allow this model of classroom management to be constructed in a way that is illuminating for teachers in practical situations.

Even so, an exact operationalization of benefit may not be necessary if we are to focus, for example, on qualitative differences between the unruly classroom and the revolutionary classroom. We might look for evidence as to how stable or unstable the equilibrium positions were in any case, possibly by examining the functioning of the classroom when a particular child with challenging behaviour is either present or absent. Similarly, we might look at efforts by teachers to move the equilibrium position of their classroom, by explicitly adopting modified systems of rewards and punishments as suggested by the model. Such procedures would give an improved understanding of how such a model might operate and indicate areas for further improvement or modification.

In the same way, one might look at the supposed benefit structures where defection was seen to be desirable, as in contributing to a discussion in a seminar. Can an experienced seminar leader who sets up their reward structure as a revolution find a way of encouraging discussion to the point where it feeds upon itself and takes off and everybody is participating? Or are they left with a rather desultory effort to make one or two contribute, always withering away to embarrassed silence on the left-hand side of the diagram? Or does the seminar leader instead manage to generate an unruly set-up with a proportion of the group taking part in discussion and the majority remaining quiet and listening to the contributions made by the few? And can such a seminar leader find a mechanism to move that equilibrium towards the right, so that more and more people take part in the discussion? Such questions might as easily be raised in the context of e-learning and online forums as they are about face-to-face seminars. The question of individual participation in adult education is always an important one, and a method to explore ways of encouraging more people to participate would be an extremely important aspect of managing adult education.

Time and again in educational settings we find ourselves in situations where we witness either vicious cycles of degeneration into riot or silence, or virtuous cycles of escalation into silence or animated discussion (depending upon our teaching goals and perspectives). Although we can clearly see that individuals feed off the atmosphere and encouragement of the group as a whole, we are not always clear what it is that we have done, or that others have done, to send the group into ascent or descent along the path it is taking. What I have set out here is a possible model for exploring how the decisions made by individuals within a group in an educational setting may so influence each other that the outcome is both independent of but created by the individual choices of participants. What is more, if the models work they also contain within them the recommendations of the qualities which could be employed to try to move from one situation to another. Whether such models work in practice is of course open to question, and it is a question that needs to be examined more fully on a empirical basis.

In this case, as in the other cases presented in this book, I am suggesting the start of a research agenda not the end of it. The models set out here have an appropriate form to accommodate different arrangements and different policies in classroom management. In that sense they offer a way of examining classroom management in some detail and with some sophistication. In terms of Einstein's dictum that theory should be as simple as possible but no simpler, the models I have presented here are still extraordinarily simple when compared with the multitude of interactions that happen within the classroom, but they are less simple than some of the models of teacher behaviour that we currently have and use in research. Current models, as has been noted, suggest that teacher interventions are conducted as a series of separate, dyadic relationships between the teacher and a single pupil. Whether the models presented here, when combined with empirical observations of how teachers actually structure rewards for their pupils in their classes, can prove to be practically useful is a question that can only be addressed through further research.

Prior research

Classroom management is an important topic for trainee teachers and newly qualified teachers. It looks as though it ought to be of immense practical import for the new teacher, offering insight into the most crucial question of all, how to survive the next 45 minutes.

Long ago, when I first started teaching, the seasoned teachers in school used to give new teachers four pieces of advice (they probably still do). Do not lose your temper. Do not make threats that you do not intend to follow through (or cannot follow through). Do not punish a whole class for the misdeeds of a few. And start off very strict at the beginning (preferably line the class up outside the classroom and have them quiet before they go into the room in good order). There were two main principles underlying this advice. The first was that now was the time to disabuse the young teacher of any idea that theory was of any use in the real world of the classroom. And the second was that it was easier to relax discipline later, but in that first phase, when teacher and pupils are sounding each other out, it was unwise to give too much away too early.

Like most novice teachers, I did my best to ignore the advice, and in that way learned how sound it was as a starting point. It amounted, in very brief outline, to the instructions as to how to set up the reward structure identified above as the perfect classroom. What is needed is a consistent set of rewards and punishments, according to which each child would know that they would receive their just deserts in the light of their behaviour (i.e. they would not be punished for the misdeeds of others). For the reward structure to be credible and consistent it was important that there should be no empty threats, and not losing one's temper was the key to consistency.

But the advice included the overtone of something else: that inexorable law of the classroom that discipline can deteriorate, but once the teacher has lost that magic whatever-it-is, there will be no climbing back up the slippery slope. Or, if there is, it will be a long hard climb. Classroom management is not just a question of the here and now, the rewards and punishments; there is something in the history of the group, the confidence of the way the teacher does things, something which is about the dynamics of the group which is not captured in the one-to-one relationship of the teacher with each of the pupils individually.

Studies of classroom management abound, but they rarely move far beyond the 'tips and tricks' approach that was embodied in that knowing advice from experienced teachers that I received before first going into the classroom. An earlier example of such studies can be found in Fontana (1994: 3) who also makes clear what the focus of such studies has been: 'This book is about applying psychological principles and insights to the business of controlling and managing a class of children.' Although Fontana adds a number of caveats about how 'control' should be understood, that he is not advocating a return to Victorian rigidity, his focus is very clearly on the psychology of individuals, and not on the sociology of group interactions. Moreover, while he makes clear that 'misbehaviour' and 'lack of discipline' arise from the social context and are framed by teacher behaviour, nevertheless he returns again and again to discussion of the dyadic relationship between a teacher and a single child.

In fact, Fontana (1994: 158–60) steps out of this model at only one point, to describe a 'class out of control' – not arising from any internal dynamics, of course, but a class left unattended, and taking advantage of the opportunity for some good-natured fun. But again, the teacher is advised to identify children whom he or she would expect to respond positively, and single them out by name. There is no consideration of interactions between fellow pupils.

More recent volumes have incorporated models of leadership and management which imply a more sociological approach, but in practice much of the material emphasizes interactions and conversations between a teacher and an individual pupil, and how a teacher can manage such exchanges, giving the pupil time and space in which to conform without loss of dignity. For example, Rogers (2002) offers a collection of such perspectives.

Wolfgang (2001) provides a survey of approaches to classroom management, ranging from behavioural and cognitive approaches, which clearly have roots in psychology, to policies based in assertive discipline and whole-school policies. However, even then, it is noticeable that all of the 'classroom discipline vignettes' he offers at the end of the volume (Wolfgang 2001: 263–6) involve the description of the behaviour of a single pupil or student in a setting where everything, apart from the background of the individual and the actions of the teacher, are irrelevant.

This is unsatisfactory for two reasons. In the first place, what novice teachers need more than anything else are the tools to analyse what went wrong. When they come out of that nightmare classroom that we have all occasionally faced, they need to understand exactly how they might have managed it differently. And they need to know what to do next time in order to re-establish relationships that have been damaged and reputations that have been tarnished. Those are the classroom-management tools that novices really need.

And as they gain more experience and more confidence, they need a second set of tools, to tell them how to manage experiments, how to take their classes nearer to the edge of the abyss so that the learning is genuinely risky and memorable. How can they recognize when they are on the verge of going too far? How can they bring the class away from dangerous situations again? And how can they play the group's dynamics and feelings as professionals should be able to – as, say, musicians or actors might?

The static advice to be consistent to the point of boredom, not to let emotion enter into decisions and to be strict for fear that the worst might happen all constitute sound advice, but in the long-run they gradually destroy the excitement of teaching. We all know teachers who have a reputation for being strict. Their classes run like clockwork. But precisely because they run according to plan, nothing very exciting ever happens in them. Neither teacher nor learners have very much fun, although the teacher may be held in very high regard: 'Mr X is a good teacher; he makes us work hard and we get a lot of work done.' Neat notebooks, plenty of notes, lots of exercises finished and marked correct, but not much love of learning or management of self-control.

What teachers need is a dynamic set of tools that allow them to manage classrooms in a way that suits their own professional development. What would happen if I set up the classroom today as a revolutionary situation, and used the energy that underlies that setting to inspire a debate and motivate learning? Would I know how to manage that, and how to use the situation I have created?

There is a strong temptation to want to go back into classrooms again and try to recapture that excitement of being a new teacher. Knowing what I know now, could I go back and actually achieve the things that I hoped to achieve then? But, of course, that is impossible. Apart from anything else, I am older, and I look older, which means that classes would react to me differently. And on top of that, I know the most important thing that one learns about teaching through experience, that teachers generally survive even their worst lessons. And that confidence weighs very heavily in favour of the experienced teacher. So can we use models from multiperson game theory which support the understanding of classroom management for teachers at all stages of their development, and does this reduce teachers to the status of teaching machines?

Future directions for research

The multiperson game-theory models that I have been looking at suggest that there are qualitative differences between different classroom settings. The anecdotal evidence suggests that one can tell the difference between an unruly classroom and a revolution in the sense that one has a level of suppressed energy that the other does not. But this needs to be explored further. Does such a classification of different settings actually hold up if one analyses what happens in classrooms from a qualitative perspective? Do teachers describe different goals in terms of classroom management? There is a good deal that could be explored here, simply in the terms that teachers and learners use to describe their classroom experiences.

However, beyond that, the models of multiperson game theory also suggest possible areas for quantitative research. The models suppose that 'rewards and punishments' can be relatively easily identified and evaluated. Yet we know that real classrooms are more complex than that. Many different kinds of rewards exist in a classroom.

Teachers are vulnerable to being wound up. They know a lot about their subject, and they are in the classroom because they love to explain it. And they are aware of many little subtleties of argument and failings that the novice may not yet fully have understood. But what 14- and 15-year-olds understand only too well is that if the teacher can be manoeuvred into an area where they find the explanation full of unspoken complexities, and if they can be flustered and rushed a little bit, they can be led off the topic they planned to talk about, and probably confused and annoyed as well, without anybody having done anything worse than having shown an interest in the subject and asked a few awkward questions. What could be more rewarding than that?

Well, for a start there may be a gold star, a good mark in red pen, a glowing end-of-term report, or a successful outcome in the end-of-year examination. How do these different rewards stack up one against the other? Can they be converted in some way? (Embarrassing the teacher in front of your mates is worth three gold stars?) Or are different learners motivated by different rewards? (The learner who cares about gold stars is not likely to be affected by what his mates think, and vice versa.) When a teacher walks into the classroom, are they managing one group of 30 learners, or two groups (boys and girls perhaps), or more?

These practical questions about whether and how the motivations of different learners operate are exactly the areas where future work could be focused. The models from multiperson game theory open up a new range of questions, and although the models may be immediately suggestive of some new mechanisms for understanding classroom management, many of the details remain rather sketchy, and are bound to until further empirical work has been carried out. This is where future research should go.

Chapter 6

The Parting of the Ways

Introduction

The second area that I have chosen for examining the possibilities offered by multicentred models of educational research is career choice. This might be a choice whether to stay on at school at 16, or to study a particular subject at university, or any of other numerous points at which the path through educational institutions bifurcate.

The first assumption that underpins a multicentred approach is that the observed fact that a group divides itself between the options must make some kind of sense, serve some kind of purpose. This will not necessarily be the purpose of any individual involved, but in some greater scheme of things it must make sense. There is a difficulty conveying what is intended here; one of the points which I will return to again and again is that the sum of individual purposes, the way in which the actions of individuals add together, may result in group behaviour and general outcomes which nobody intended. In this sense, the way in which working-class children move away from higher education may not be in line with government policy. It may also be possible to point to individuals who have gone from working-class backgrounds into higher education and have done very well. But at some level, the general under-representation of working-class people in higher education must have some function; the methodological assumption of a multicentred approach is that no group of people is so stupid that they would persist in actions which are without any function.

If we think of the case of the choice to stay on at school into post-compulsory education at the end of compulsory schooling we can get a sense of what is involved. If every young person chose to stay on in school and pursue an academic education, we can see what the consequences would be. There would be very high levels of competition for university places and for eventual employment in the professions. Many of those choosing to invest in academic education would subsequently be rejected by institutions or employers, and would ultimately be forced into jobs where their qualifications were of no value, or did not bring any special reward. The investment would not bring any return, and those individuals might well come to see their education as 'wasted'. At the same time, there would be a shortage of applicants for training in practical trades, for running errands for businesses, or for performing unpleasant and manual tasks. Such trades and occupations would command a premium because of the shortage of those willing to do them. This would increase the opportunity costs of post-compulsory education, as those who stayed on in education would be forgoing income which could be earned outside. There would be an incentive for a number of young people to move away from academic education and into manual employment.

In contrast with that, if we consider the opposite scenario, where every young person chose to leave formal education at the earliest opportunity, there would be excessive competition for manual work, and shortages in the professions. There would be every incentive for some individuals to change their minds and pursue their education, confident that they would be guaranteed a place in institutions of higher learning, and that they would not face competition in their chosen professions.

Somewhere between these two hypothetical scenarios must be a position where some young people choose to stay in post-compulsory education and others choose to leave. At a level where there is some competition for advancement on both career paths, there will be no incentive for an individual to switch from their chosen path to the other. In that situation it would make sense to think of the system as being in equilibrium, with individuals on both educational trajectories feeling that they are doing the best for themselves that they can.

It is clear that at one level the options which are available to each individual are shaped by the decisions of every other member of the cohort making a similar choice; if more people choose the academic route, this will increase the competition along that path and reduce likely returns. But at the same time, each individual facing the choice is equal, in the sense that each makes a choice in ignorance of what everybody else will do; each individual needs to confront her own career choice on her own, and use her reason and feeling the best she can. But her choice will also be made in the absence of much important information; she will be ignorant of what everybody else is doing.

In this way, although the career choices being considered here are intimately connected with the choices that everybody else makes, they are less intimately connected than the choices of pupils in a classroom setting. In that case each pupil could sit and wait, to see how the teacher reacts to the undisciplined behaviour of his friend, perhaps even manoeuvre his friend out into the open to test the teacher's reaction, before deciding how he is going to conduct himself. In the case of a career choice, the commitment has to be made before the behaviour of others can be observed.

It might be possible to use the same analytical methods to describe career choice as have been demonstrated for classroom management, and at some time in the future that may be desirable, but as a first attempt at modelling career choice in a multicentred way I propose to use a rather simpler model, that of a two-person zero-sum game against Nature.

I hope that even at this point, the explanation of why there is likely to be an equilibrium solution of any career choice, with individuals distributing themselves between the various options available, will prompt numerous speculations. Can the choice really only be about money? What about people who report that they 'had no choice'? Can the equilibrium be moved? And if it can, can it be moved simply by enlarging (reducing the competition for) educational institutions? Or does it need changes in the labour-market and other societal institutions? I shall return to some of these questions, and others, later. If they have risen to mind immediately, then I would suggest that is at least an indication of the fruitfulness of multicentred approaches to research; no sooner has such a model been conceived than it stimulates many possible lines of future research. However, before embarking on some of that speculation, it would be better to articulate with more precision the model that is going to be used in this chapter.

Two-person zero-sum games against Nature

A two-person zero-sum game, as the name implies, is a game in which there are two players, each of whom makes a choice of strategy before a play of the game starts, and where the outcome of the play is that one or other of the players wins. A draw is not ruled out, but the important point is that the loser pays the winner; what the winner wins is exactly the same as what the loser loses. There can be no grounds for collaboration between the players, and consequently these games are sometimes referred to as strictly competitive games. Before going on to the complications that arise when one player is Nature, some of the theoretical results from ordinary two-person games are important to the development of this model.

Two players, A and B, are each to place a penny coin on the table in front of them, but without the other seeing whether they are placed down with the head or the tail showing. When they have both placed their coin, they disclose their coin to the other. If the coins are both the same, A wins. If they are different, B wins. The winner takes both coins. This is a two-person zero-sum game, where each player chooses between heads (H) and tails (T).

The amount that A wins (and by implication B loses) can be shown in a simple table, known as a pay-off matrix.

A game may be very much more complex than this, and appear to have a sequence of moves, and yet be capable of representation as a simple two-person zero-sum game. For example, the game of noughts and crosses appears to have a sequence of moves. On a three by three grid of nine squares, the player with crosses (who always plays first) has to choose between putting the first cross in the centre square, a corner square or a square in the middle of a side. (Because the grid is symmetrical, these are the only three choices.) The player playing noughts must then choose one of eight responses, by placing a nought in an empty square. The player of crosses then responds with a second cross, at which point it should be clear whether the game will be a draw, or if not which of the players will win.

At the start of the game, the player who starts with crosses should select the strategy, 'Place a cross in a corner. If the other player puts a nought in the centre square, put a cross in the opposite corner; otherwise put a cross in the centre square.' The result is that the player with crosses who chooses this strategy can never lose, and will give him or herself the best chance of winning.

In this way, a pay-off matrix can provide for the players to make a selection from among several strategies, and a relatively complex set of preferences can be accommodated.

Game theorists suspect that chess is a game of this sort, where there is a strategy that white (the player to move first) could choose, and from which the result of the game would follow, but because of the range of choices and the number of steps taken in the process of a game, nobody has yet been able to construct the pay-off matrix, much less solve it and work out how a game of chess should best be played.

Game theory covers the solution of such games; this involves working out what each player should do to optimize her results. This involves anticipating what the opponent will do to optimize her results, and then choosing between those options which the actions of the opponent make available. Since the opponent will not choose a course of action which invariably leads to a loss for her, there is no point selecting a course of action which depends upon that altruism from the opponent. This sequence of looking for the best outcome while the opponent tries to minimize your options is described in the literature as a mini-max solution. This is at the heart of the difference from single-centred solutions which invariably look at the simple maximization of benefits.

In the simple game represented in Figure 6.1 we can see with relatively little reflection that if player B were always to pick the same strategy,

		Choice made by A	
		H	T
Choice made by B	H	+1	−1
	T	−1	+1

Figure 6.1 Simple pay-off matrix

player A could easily adjust her response so that she always won. Indeed, the essence of selecting a successful strategy in such a game is that one should not be predictable; the player who wants to win such a game must mix choices, in predictable proportions in the long-run, but in such a way that any single play is unpredictable. This is known as a mixed strategy, and is contrasted with a pure strategy, such as the one which crosses should play in a game of noughts and crosses.

From a qualitative perspective, solutions of two-person games have a number of interesting features. In the first place, mini-max solutions usually involve the player in either a pure strategy or a mixed strategy made up of a combination of two pure strategies. That is to say that a two-person game model can be used to describe a situation in which everybody who plays the game should always make the same choice (a single-centred solution). However, more frequently players should choose a mixed strategy made up of two pure strategies played in a sequence where the long-run proportion of each is fixed but where any single play is unpredictable.

A second important feature of the solutions of two-person games is that players should avoid risky options, or more precisely, in a mixed strategy, the strategy that has outcomes that are closer together should be played with greater frequency. We can see how this works if we look at the game pay-off matrix in Figure 6.2, a modification of the game set out in Figure 6.1. In this case the game has been modified to make the outcome when both players play heads much more attractive for A.

An application of maximizing logic suggests that A should play heads much more frequently, in order to increase the likelihood of such a win. But

		Choice made by A	
		H	T
Choice made by B	H	+5	−1
	T	−1	+1

Figure 6.2 Modified pay-off matrix

the application of mini-max logic brings us to the opposite conclusion; B will be extremely interested in avoiding the double heads outcome, and will therefore choose tails much more frequently than odds. Armed with the information that B is much more likely to play tails, then A should also play tails more frequently than heads in order to maximize the likelihood that A and B will play the same. By putting a much higher value on the win that A secures when both players play heads, the likelihood that A will win is increased, and the average expectation of gain for A (the value of the game) goes up. But paradoxically, A achieves this result by avoiding the very attractive outcome.

And a third important qualitative result is that if A has chosen her mini-max strategy, then the amount she can expect to win, the value of the game, is exactly the same whatever the strategy that B chooses. In this case, the mini-max strategy for A is that tails should be chosen 75 per cent of the time; in 100 plays A should choose tails 75 times and heads 25 times. Having made that decision, A is completely indifferent to the choices of B. If B chooses heads 100 times, A will lose 1p on 75 occasions and win 5p on 25; a total return of 50p on 100 plays or 0.5p per play. If B chooses tails 100 times, A will win 1p on 75 occasions and lose 1p on 25; a total return of 50p on 100 plays or 0.5p per play. And if B chooses any combination of heads and tails, A can still expect a return of 0.5p per play. Of course, an astute player A could anticipate B's weaknesses if B plays a sub-optimum strategy, and A would be able to do better than 0.5p per play by exploiting B's inadequacies. The mini-max strategy represents a kind of 'insurance policy' which gives a steady return whatever the opponent chooses to do.

Games against Nature

If we take the example of the choice made by 16-year-olds to stay on in education or to leave and go out to work, it is clear that the individuals who make that choice do so with only partial knowledge. They may know very well that continuing their education will lead to certain possibilities − university, professional work, white-collar employment − and that leaving education for work will lead to others. They may even, if they are particularly well informed, have information at their fingertips on likely occupations, lifetime earning streams and pensions. But there will be many other aspects of that choice, particularly future choices of others, which are incapable of being known. Will they do well in their studies? Will they get good grades in their exams? Will they get places on the courses and in the institutions they wish? Will the competition for employment be high? Will they end up in a dead-end job with no prospects? Will they find opportunities for self-development and self-fulfilment?

In terms of modelling that choice, we might think of an impersonal opponent, a fickle fate, or, as is more common in the literature, Nature. In the UK, a million young people each year reach the age of 16, and each of them has to choose between staying on at school or leaving school behind and entering employment. For each of them Nature puts a card in a sealed envelope, which says which path will bring them success: 'You will be successful if you go out of school and into employment, but unsuccessful if you stay on at school', or vice versa. Each young person must choose, in a million plays of the game, whether to stay on at school or leave, without knowing what is in the sealed envelope. It is as though player A in Figure 6.2 knew what the outcomes of playing heads or tails might be, but without having any idea what player B would do, and hence whether the outcome would be the higher or lower pay-off from A's choice.

But, of course, that is exactly how A does play the game. A knows what the contents of each cell of the pay-off matrix contains, but in the absence of knowledge about what B will do, cannot know with precision what the outcome will be on any single play. We might therefore hope to model the choices of 16-year-olds as a game against a fictional player, Nature, who will make a decision which will affect the eventual outcome.

I do not particularly want to focus on the player Nature. When A plays against player B, the best solution is to pick the mini-max solution. Once the mini-max solution has been chosen, A gains the same amount from the game, whatever player B chooses to do. There is a logic to the structure of the game and the mini-max solution that makes the responses of the actual player B almost irrelevant. Only if player B chooses to play in particularly foolish ways and is explicitly predictable does A need to consider the personal disposition of B. In all other circumstances, A can secure her own position by employing the mini-max solution, and the personality of B is irrelevant. In much the same way, I am going to argue that Nature is irrelevant. Knowing the best and the worst that can happen to her by following either course of action, A can choose the mini-max solution which will protect her against the vagaries of Nature. Unpacking what Nature is like will not be necessary, unless one of the elements that I have chosen to wrap up under the general construct of 'Nature' makes an explicit attempt to change how we view the format of the game; if a government policy to guarantee a university place to everybody who wanted it was introduced, for example.

But, as in Figure 6.2, player A was encouraged by the mini-max strategy to avoid the option that gave the widest range of risk, so in playing against Nature, the options which involve the greatest risk will be avoided. It should be noted here that in the context of a mini-max solution of a two-person game, the word 'risk' has a very specific meaning. In game theory, risk is the difference between a good outcome and a bad outcome.

In everyday language, 'risk' is normally taken to mean simply something unpleasant. Before I travel abroad my employer asks me to complete a 'risk assessment'. I am invited to identify anything that could go disastrously wrong, and to suggest steps that have been taken to ensure that it does not happen. At which point, presumably, it stops being a risk, and the whole exercise would become futile, had it not been so from the beginning. This is a foolish way of conceptualizing risk, and is both rooted in single-centredness (every outcome is knowable) and a lack of logic (if a bad outcome is avoidable, it is no longer a risk). In game theory, risk cannot be avoided altogether, since whichever path we adopt, the difference between a good and a bad outcome cannot be avoided. We can only choose a path where the difference is smaller.

The point of this brief discussion of risk is to highlight some possibilities that this way of modelling choice highlights. If a game-theory model of a game against Nature is an effective way of modelling young people's choices, then it suggests that there is a need to take into account the circumstances surrounding both choices. Individuals will not be trying to maximize their returns, but to manage their risk using a mini-max strategy. Policies which aim to emphasize the best outcome of a particular course of action (stressing the putative benefits of staying on at school, for example), or even to exaggerate them, may be counterproductive if the result is to emphasize the distance between the best and the worst outcomes. Policies designed to increase the best outcome ('golden hellos' or entry incentives) may also be counterproductive, or less effective than policies designed to improve the worst outcome (a minimum wage, for example). Approaches to the management of choice which appear obvious and intuitive from the perspective of individuals who are seeking to maximize their returns at any cost may seem pointless from the perspective of individuals who are trying to manage their risk rather than maximize returns.

Anecdotal evidence

I have chosen to develop two-person zero-sum games against Nature as a possible model for educational choice because it chimes with my personal experience of educational choices. Quite apart from the general considerations of multicentredness that I set out in Chapter 2, there are, in my view, specific reasons for choosing such a model of educational choice.

I do not, as it happens, remember having made a conscious choice at the age of 16; my education up to the age of 18 was focused upon a grammar school and the determination and expectation on the part of all concerned that university was the ultimate destination. At the age of 18, however, I made two important educational choices, the choice of university to apply to and the choice of subject to study.

On the question of university, I was quite clear. I wanted most of all to attend an ancient university with an impeccable tradition. But my reason for wanting this was not about maximizing returns or seeking the maximum anything. As I recall my reasoning was that if, after three years of under-graduate study, I was disappointed with the experience, I would not regret my choice or reproach myself that there were better places that I could have gone to study. And that turned out to be prescient. The experience of study-ing engineering at Cambridge was pretty dire, as much for what I brought to the experience as any shortcomings of Cambridge (of which there were many). But in the 30 years since, I have never thought that I would have been better off studying at a different institution, even if in fact I would have been.

And then there was the question of subject choice. At school I delighted in mathematics and physics, and in learning for its own sake. The obvi-ous choice was, perhaps, physics at undergraduate level. And I think that I would have chosen that but for a lack of confidence. I knew, I suppose everybody knows, what successful physicists do. They become Einstein, or Buckminster-Fuller or Cavendish. But what do unsuccessful physicists become? On the other hand, successful engineers designed glamorous pro-jects such as bridges and tall buildings and high dams. But there were plenty of jobs for less successful engineers, in designing, building and main-taining public-sector works, such as sewage plants and water-treatment installations. Although I had a rather different set of priorities when I decided to leave engineering behind forever three years later, at the age of 18 engineering looked a better bet to me, because the management of risk seemed to be more possible for somebody who did not make the top grade.

Memory is, of course, a notoriously poor way of collecting data about choices and thoughts from 30 years ago, and quite probably I have overlaid the original raw material with interpretations and some colouring based upon theories that I would like to be applicable. But it seems to me that both choices contained an important element of risk management, of avoid-ing courses of action where something truly regrettable might happen, how-ever brightly the possible prizes shone.

This prompts a speculation to which I will return later. In part, this offers an explanation as to why individuals tend to end up in careers which are fairly close to those of their parents. I perceived the career of physicist to be riskier than that of engineer. In fact, the risk in either could be relatively easily managed by taking up a career in teaching, as I eventually did; one was probably not much riskier than the other. But the appearance of risk may be highly subjective, and one is likely to know more about those second-choice options if one has some personal knowledge of people who have worked in that area. The avoidance of apparent risk might be a potent force in the reproduction of social-class patterns of employment, and knowledge might be a powerful tool in promoting social mobility.

By the mid-1970s I was a teacher of physics in secondary schools, and trying to dispense some of that information about future life-chances to my pupils. And I was struck by the fact that no young person ever seemed to be making what they thought was a wrong choice. We had our normal crop of young boys who intended to be pop stars or football millionaires, and therefore had scant interest in school. But I remember particularly one 15-year-old who had decided to leave school to go out to work. His plan included his establishment of a taxi firm, and that by the time he was 25 he would 'Earn much more than you do now, Sir' (the word 'Sir' being imbued with the full weight of our relative financial success in his eyes).

At the same time, one of the things that I disliked about those years was the fact that girls rarely wanted to study physics, and that seemed to me to be a pity, partly from the point of view of their future prospects, but mainly because I found that single-sex classes of either sex were less civilized than mixed classes. There were a few girls, of course, who studied physics. But for the most part they were very able, and had their sights set on a career in veterinary science or medicine. There seemed to be, in the popular culture, a lack of those second-choice options which would allow girls to control the risk within a science-based career. Fortunately career patterns have changed a good deal, and I think that career stereotyping is less marked than it was at that time, but then it seemed that science was a very risky choice for young women.

These various experiences seemed to me to be at least somewhat illuminated by modelling them as a game against Nature. The paradox that group behaviour should be fairly predictable, while individuals would often surprise one, and that individuals always had a positive spin to put on their choices, seemed to be mirrored in the game-theoretical position that a long series of plays was predicted in theory, but the essence of the single play was to be unpredictable. Indeed, in spite of attempts in the literature, and my attempt here, to bring the game-theory analysis to bear upon individual experience, there is some doubt as to whether a game-theory analysis can be applied to a single play at all.

I was, however, persuaded by the need for an understanding of mixed strategies, which I have generalized here into a multicentred approach. It seemed to me wrong that we should stigmatize those who chose to leave education as 'failures' or 'drop-outs'. They generally seemed to have weighed their options up very carefully and could always put forward a positive account of their choice. It seemed to me to be important to look for theories that would explain both why some young people stay on in education and why some leave it. Hitherto, theorists have only sought to explain one or the other, to find the difference which defines and separates those who drop out from those who do not.

I have also wondered, from time to time, whether the fact that a mini-max strategy will normally incorporate at most two pure strategies has any power in explaining why, in England, only academic and general secondary schools (grammar schools and secondary modern) have been successful, and until recently the system has proved particularly resistant to the introduction of a third type (most obviously technical schools). However, that speculation must wait for another time.

Some years ago I was sitting at a table outside the students' union bar on the campus of a former polytechnic. A young woman came and sat down at the same table, and started talking about the decision that she was trying to make. She had studied for two years of a degree programme but had left the course at that point with a diploma, rather than completing her degree. With her qualifications she had secured a good job as a skilled secretary/administrator in a professional practice. Now she was trying to decide whether she should return to university to obtain her degree, and achieve higher status as a professional. 'I just wanted,' she said, 'to soak up the university atmosphere for a while, to decide whether I wanted to come back to study. It is difficult to decide whether to give up a well-paid job in order to complete my degree.'

The career choice that the young woman faced was clear enough. She was going to have to invest a considerable amount in obtaining a degree, in terms of time, effort and forgone earnings. However, she could see that if she did have a degree she would have a more satisfying job, but that she might have to take on additional responsibilities and commitments if she wished to be successful and earn more. She was facing not a fixed choice but a risky choice in which she could make some decisions, but the eventual outcome would depend on a range of circumstances that were not within her control. This looked to me like a situation that could be understood in terms of a game against Nature. Incidentally, I thought that it was interesting and suggestive that she had worked in a professional practice and gained experience of what that choice was about before coming back to ponder her options. She may not have had experience of what professionals do before she was in a position to work closely with them, and her work as an administrator may have given her valuable information about how to manage the risks involved. But the task that she was involved in was clearly about handling a decision with partial knowledge.

I was shocked, however, that she was choosing to sit with me outside the students' union bar 'to soak up the university atmosphere'. As I cast my eyes across the urban setting in front of us, the redbrick, technology college building, the goods-loading bay, the storage tanks for the central heating oil and the backs of workshops that had seen better days, I could not help thinking that there were a thousand other places that I would have thought more redolent of university atmosphere than that spot. The dreaming spires of Oxford it most definitely was not.

On the other hand, the ancient universities hold other problems for working-class students. While they are learning how to study at this level and to manage their own learning (possibly for the first time) they are also having to learn a lot of other social skills of mixing with people from very different backgrounds, who carry themselves with a certain assurance. State secondary schools may offer an excellent intellectual grounding in the basic elements of the disciplines that they teach, but they do not necessarily confer the confidence inspired by living in a privileged family, or teach the range of social interests and manners cultivated by living in a boarding school.

And here we have the basic paradox of any system of voluntary segregation, that it takes only quite limited or weak preferences on the part of individuals to be in environments where a substantial minority of those that I meet will be something like me, for the whole system to become completely and irrevocably segregated. For a female working-class student from an ethnic minority background an urban ex-polytechnic was exotic enough to come to terms with, was the embodiment of 'university atmosphere', without the additional difficulties of coming to terms with other dimensions of class and privilege. In that sense, admissions tutors who claim that their intake is biased because applications are biased, are absolutely correct. There is a process of self-selection going on here that creates student bodies and an institutional ethos with which people are comfortable. But does it provide equality of opportunity? (This question is examined in more detail in Chapter 7.)

In this chapter I have set out a model of career choice as a 'game against Nature'. But I have also hinted that there might be scope for looking at career choice as a multiperson game of the sort described in Chapter 5, where the choices of all participants contributed to the environment in which each person made their own choice. In the former model, the person under consideration is presumed to make a choice in a constant environment but with limited information, while in the latter they are presumed to be in an environment which changes as others make their choices.

So which of those two phenomena predominates: is university choice a career decision made with limited information, or is it a group action in which the choices each applicant makes are shaped by the anticipation that their peers are also making certain choices? The simple answer is that we do not know for certain. The best that we can do is to develop models of the career decision to enter higher education, and see how much of the choice can be explained in those terms. Similarly, we can develop models of the selection of university ethos, and the interaction of individual choices, and of selecting institutions with a student body that will be 'something like me', and see how much of the decision that might explain. Only when we have developed both of those strands can we realistically address the question of which predominates.

Prior research

Previous research on career choice has fallen into one of two main patterns, that people have 'traits' that suit them to particular kinds of work, and that people have background factors which predispose them to particular routes through the process of work selection. Traits will include personal characteristics, such as enjoying working with people, or hating working indoors, which can be matched up to characteristics of jobs. Factors may be elements in a person's background history, such as being the youngest of a number of siblings, which are not strictly personality traits but which may have an impact on career choices. However, in previous research career choice, *qua* choice, has not been explicitly built into the models used.

An example of the factor approach can be found in Gambetta's (1987) book, *Were They Pushed or Did They Jump?*. As the title suggests, the premise of this book is that there is an interesting area to examine, whether individuals can or cannot make meaningful choices that are oriented towards future aims, or whether their behaviour is an epiphenomenon of stronger social currents. However, if we look at the way in which Gambetta approaches this question, we can see the weaknesses of single-centred thinking.

Gambetta takes various background variables and feeds them into a 'logit' model to predict whether individuals will stay on in education or not. Since all the variables are entered into the same statistical process, the model is actually incapable of differentiating between 'push' and 'jump' factors. Any such differentiation depends upon an interpretation of what the factors mean.

For example, Gambetta (1987: 109–13) argues that 'father's age' can be used as a proxy for future financial difficulties (with the retirement of the parents) and that the fact that 'father's age' can be used to discriminate between those who will and those who will not stay on at school indicates that young people are capable of anticipating future constraints (and therefore of making anticipatory decisions to jump). But without changing the statistical analysis at all, we could equally argue that 'father's age' was a push factor, a background variable that made the young person vulnerable to leaving school, equivalent, for example, to the parent's highest educational qualification. The latter is not supposed to be something that the young person anticipates, but it affects their education, possibly by affecting the interest that the parent shows in the child's performance at school.

In Gambetta's models there are only independent variables and dependent variables. Distinguishing between the independent variables, as between those that show structural constraints and those that show freedom of choice, is not a matter of statistical analysis; it is a matter of the gloss put on that analysis by Gambetta. Much the same argument would apply to any multivariate, regression or discriminant analysis model that could be chosen. The models are not sophisticated enough to produce evidence either for or against the efficacy of individual choice.

This example shows the overall weakness of such 'factor' approaches. There is the further difficulty that any such factors that might be identified are stochastic, and therefore factors cannot be identified as causes, but in some intangible way they combine to produce the results observed. By no means does every person who has elderly parents end up taking the same career path.

Similar arguments can be made about traits: not everybody who loves working in the great outdoors actually ends up doing so. Career choice is a purposeful balance between background experience and knowledge, future anticipation and luck (or reliance upon partial information). Game theory allows that combination to be modelled explicitly. Its absence leads to models that are excessively simplistic. Career education is therefore based on attempting to match what is known about the person with what is known about the demands of particular occupations. This means that the reflective, self-directing, anticipatory aspects of the process are overlooked. As Law (1996: 47) has noted, 'At its simplest this is "pegs-and-holes" thinking.' But at the same time, Law expresses the need to go beyond this to develop a theory of the reflective learner about one's own personal history.

Killeen (1996: 34) argues that 'Careers theory has to attempt to bridge the gap between the two – between universality and history.' This is the same tension that I have noted in saying that educational theory needs to be able to accommodate understanding at different levels, between individuals and institutions, without the one defining the other. Killeen, therefore, comes to a conclusion that career theory has been trying to incorporate two different aspects, but that because the elements the career theorists put together may not be compatible, this may be an obstacle to future development. I take this to be an indication that theorists within the field of careers and careers education have identified a similar need for the development of theory to the one that I argue for here.

There is a need, generally, to acknowledge, as I argued in the first chapter of this book, that career decisions and career education are not something set apart from the rest of education, but that they are part of the way in which an individual produces his or her own identity. And in that process, there is no mechanical passing of identity or culture from one individual to another, of from one generation to the next. Personal identity is made up from pieces that we choose to integrate into our own identity in a process which can broadly be characterized as 'education'.

And certainly, there is a recognition in the literature that individuals can reject or adapt what is offered to them; they do not merely need to accept what is put forward. This is captured in the idea of 'resistance'. For example, Satterthwaite *et al.* (2006) record a number of ways in which such resistance can be observed.

Of particular interest in this respect is the chapter by Honan (2006). Honan takes the notion of bricolage from Levi-Strauss, via Derrida.

> The bricoleur, says Levi-Straus, is someone who uses 'the means at hand', that is the instruments he finds at his disposition around him, those which are already there, and which had not been especially conceived with an eye to the operation for which they are to be used and to which one tries by trial and error to adapt them, not hesitating to change them whenever it appears necessary, or to try several of them at once, even if their form and origin are heterogeneous. (Derrida 1978: 285)

Levi-Strauss contrasts the *bricoleur* with the engineer, 'A subject who supposedly would be the absolute origin of his own discourse, and supposedly would construct it "out of nothing", "out of whole cloth" ...' (Derrida 1978: 285).

Derrida's discussion is set in the context of scientific method, a notion that rests on the myth of objectivity rooted in logical method, but which has, in fact, pulled itself up by its own bootstraps through a process of bricolage. But he notes that it is equally applicable to other spheres, such as literary criticism. Honan extends that still further by arguing that it also describes the way in which the curriculum is notionally a rational selection from the culture for education of children but in practice rests upon a patchwork of personal decisions and interpretations by individual teachers.

In the same way I wish to argue that the process of identity formation is not an engineered process whereby one inherits certain capacities and traits which shape what one becomes, nor is it engineered in the sense of being shaped by potent environmental forces, including forceful teachers. It is assembled by each individual on the shaky foundations of what has gone before.

However, I wish to counter the next possible step in the development of this argument. Derrida (1978: 287) notes, 'Nevertheless, even if one yields to the necessity of what Levi-Strauss has done, one cannot ignore its risks. If the mythological is mythomorphic, are all discourses on myths equivalent?' Or, in the present context, if identity formation is not conducted according to any set pattern, must we abandon the idea that there is any sort of pattern in identity formation? I think that Derrida intends this rhetorical question to be answered in the negative, and I would certainly respond in the negative. Identity formation is haphazard, but it is the haphazard nature of chaos or complexity, in which, nevertheless, some pattern can be discerned.

An individual may choose to learn this skill, or reject it, choose to make that ability an important element in the way she presents herself, but play down another characteristic, and she may choose to do so at will. But that does not mean to say that there is no structure. Some skills and characteristics are more likely to be adopted than others. Some, though not adopted into the personality, cannot be publicly disavowed. (We might think of the importance attached to literacy in modern society, and the stigma which still attaches to the inability to read and write.)

It is finding ways of recognizing and describing this multicentred bricolage that is at the heart of this book, and it is the sense in which game-theory models are presented as an option.

Future directions for research

I have set out some anecdotal evidence above that students whom I have met seem to be facing the kinds of choices that the game-theory models imply, and that is entirely in accord with my own memories of becoming and being an undergraduate student. There is also some indication that this is a fruitful line to follow to be found in the literature of career choice. But the empirical questions of the extent to which student choices can be explained in such terms will need further studies.

As ever, I am not suggesting here that I have the definitive answer to all of these questions. What I am suggesting is that framing career choice or educational decisions as a game against Nature or a multiperson prisoner's dilemma does allow one to develop a sophisticated and sympathetic model of the decisions that real applicants face.

To this point I have set out a two-person zero-sum game against Nature, and suggested that it might be used as a framework for analysing educational choice, as in the decision to stay on at school or leave, or to study a particular specialization. I have argued on theoretical grounds that such an approach would be attractive, and that it exemplifies how multicentred approaches might be used in this field rather than single-centred approaches that have been used until now. And I have offered some of my own experience that suggests to me, and I hope to others, that the model as set out has some merit in opening up speculation as to why we observe the phenomena we do in our educational system.

I think that I might well have multiplied those examples with others that have arisen in conversation with friends and colleagues. One of the further merits of game-theory models, from my perspective, is that they seem to prompt self-reflection, and consideration of how this understanding might frame one's representation of one's own history. And the fact that there is a distinction between group and individual analyses seems to facilitate applying the group analysis to oneself, while still leaving flexibility for one's own specific circumstances.

But I am very aware also that the point of this chapter is to show how such a model might be used to frame new research approaches, approaches that I have described as policy-based research. To that end it is important not to close down discussion by arguing that games against Nature solve all the theoretical problems *a priori* without need for further investigation. The obvious fact of the matter, but in this context very important fact, is that once one enters into speculation about multicentred approaches to career choice, one also confronts empirical questions for which we do not have answers, and for which the data is currently unavailable.

The whole body of game theory is essentially a branch of economic theory. The first and most fundamental assumption is that rational beings make choices in order to secure utilities. There is a difference from classical economic theory, that individuals are expected to select mini-max solutions rather than maximizing ones, but the fundamental issues of economic theories arise in game theory also. Is there a suitable metric for utilities that enables us to construct a framework of benefits so that we can work out what the anticipated behaviour of the population would look like? The most obvious such metric is money, and so the most simple way of asking this question is, can the behaviour of people be accounted for on the basis that they are conceived as rational planners seeking money?

I have tried this on several occasions using income figures that have been collected for other reasons in previously existing surveys (Turner 1988, 1990). The initial results have been both interesting and disappointing. They have been interesting because they suggest that people making career choices do indeed seem to move away from risk rather than towards high average, or maximum, rewards. They have been disappointing, because published data has generally been collected with a view to informing single-centred approaches, and therefore focuses on average levels of remuneration rather than ranges of risk. I have tried, in the cited study, to substitute, for example, first and third quartile earnings to illustrate the range of risk encountered in a pure strategy, but I think that a good deal more work needs to be done in characterizing pay-off matrices effectively. And much of that will be a question of what works convincingly empirically. Many decades of research have produced a great deal of data which is suitable for interrogating single-centred theories, and the base theory used shapes the data to such an extent that the data may only be imperfectly adapted to multicentred models. There is a lot of work to be done in this area.

If money is not the sole motivator for the choices that we observe, what else should be included, and how should it be incorporated alongside financial benefits? Again, this is an area where a good deal of work has been done in microeconomics, and the ways in which individuals rank their preferences has been investigated under experimental conditions. As before, most of this work has been in the context of single-centred approaches. This is not universally true, as game theory has made more of an impact on microeconomics than in most fields of the social sciences, but I have not yet seen this work extended to the area of pay-off matrices for career choice.

Even if money is the main motivator, it is not clear which money should be taken into account. I have tried taking into account earnings from longitudinal studies, that is the actual range of incomes which individuals face eight or ten years after their choice. I have also tried using labour-market figures contemporary with the choice, i.e. the information that the young people facing the choice would be able to access if they research the economic context at the time they made their choice. And I have tried to develop instruments which will elicit an image of the labour-market opportunities which the individuals believe confronts them when they make their choice. Apart from this last option, the other methods have shown some promise. Trying to develop a map of the subjective circumstances choosers face presents some difficulties of aggregating individual views, which may well take more ingenuity than I have so far exhibited. But as to which is the most effective method, I remain unconvinced that any of my methods have stood out as being obviously much better than the others. This is an area where only the development of more studies, and discussion between researchers, can produce major advances.

And this brings me to another thorny question: do people who make a career choice have to be aware of it as a rational evaluation of outcomes in order for it to be legitimate to apply a rational economic model such as game theory? My answer to this is an unqualified no. I am persuaded that a person does not have to be aware of the whole picture to fit into it. Going back to the analogy of traffic on a network of roads, so long as the traffic on my route is moving I will stick with my chosen path. If I see the traffic becoming more sluggish, I may try diverting onto an alternative route, and in that way play a small part in equalizing delays between routes. Or I may stay with my original strategy, happy in the knowledge that some people will be diverting out of the traffic jam in front of me, and so making it unnecessary for me to divert. I do not think that it is necessary for every driver to understand the structure of a game and the values in the pay-off matrix for a game-theory analysis of traffic movements to be effective. By the same token, I think that people can make their career choices on whatever basis they choose, and yet the group distribution of choices might still be optimum in terms of the group. For if they were otherwise, some individuals would have an incentive to change their choices.

However, that *a priori* response, that actors do not need to see themselves as rational agents to be usefully modelled as rational agents, does mask an issue which is open to empirical investigation. Do game-theory models predict the behaviour of groups who think of themselves as making rational choices better than groups who think of themselves as having no choice? This is a special case of a wider range of questions which can broadly be summarized: if we analyse the career choices of a million 16-year-olds a year, are we looking at one population or many? Do we need a different model for males and for females? Do we need class-specific models? Will we still need to distinguish between the population that seeks instant gratification of its desires and the population that postpones gratification? Are there other dimensions that should be used to differentiate the populations modelled in particular ways.

There remain questions that are raised by this discussion of pupil and student choices, the solution of which lies still further in the future. Throughout the discussion I have represented career-forming choices as taking place at a small number of key points – at 16, at 18, and at the end of higher education. But we all know that educational choices tend to creep up on us unawares, and rather than one big choice, we discover that we have made innumerable little choices. We forced ourselves to go to school on that day even though we had a cold, because we had a class we enjoyed. We ducked out of school on another day even though we did not really need to, because double Latin last thing on a Thursday did not really appeal. We worked harder for this teacher because they gave us a word of praise, and less hard for that one because they did not. As a result we did better in an end-of-term exam in one subject rather than another, and, as we know, nothing succeeds like success.

It might be argued that career choice is thus a much more complicated, multilayered process than I have set out here, and consequently deserves much more complicated theoretical models. I suspect that this may be true, or at least partially true. As in the example of noughts and crosses above, a 'simple' game-theory model might cover a process which in fact had several stages or steps. So when I propose a single-stage model for exploring the choices of 16-year-olds, this might be a model that brings together in concrete form all of the little choices that have been made unwittingly from the age of five to the age of 16. Or we may eventually discover that the models that I have proposed here are inadequate and in need of further refinement.

But, for the time being, I want to resist the suggestion that the models need to be more complex. I have put forward the simplest multicentred models that I can. Slightly more complex models have been used in the case of classroom management in Chapter 5, and could possibly be adapted here. Or much more complex models could be built up. For the time being, however, I rest on Occam's razor, or the principle that things should be kept as simple as possible but no simpler (a theme that I developed more fully in Chapter 2). Single-centred models are too simple for policy-based research, and so I have provided the simplest multicentred models that I can. When those models have been used to structure some research, and some data has been collected, it will be time enough to ask whether the models should be more complex in order better to represent the phenomena we wish to understand. At this moment, before much has been done in the way of empirical testing, keeping the models simple seems to be the best course of action.

This brief foray into empirical questions that would arise as one tried to apply multicentred approaches to educational choices gives some indication as to why this book is more firmly about developing a research programme and raising questions than it is about providing answers. But, as ever, the theoretical insights and the empirical questions are intimately linked. In the first place, previously collected data has for the most part been collected with the specific purpose in mind of interrogating existing theories. It may be something of a shock that such data is very well suited to the purpose for which it was collected, but can be adapted only partially to testing other theories. In fact this should not be a surprise, but is simply another manifestation of the idea that the theories that we hold set limits to what we can observe.

The other theoretical point that arises from the consideration of empirical studies is that, to date, the only way we have of deciding whether one group is underperforming is by comparing them with another. Girls underperform if they appear in particular programmes with less frequency than boys. The prospect of empirical multicentred research raises further ways of interrogating this issue. Do girls appear less frequently on certain courses as an adaptation to later opportunities (or lack of opportunities) in career paths? This may still be an indication of discrimination that we would want to remove, but would give much more precise indications of the mechanisms at work. At a time when the under-representation of working-class students in higher education is again on the agenda, and a government-funded agency to monitor fair access has been created, the possibility that such a question might be approached in a theoretically robust way ought to be welcome.

However, many of the empirical studies that have been sketched in outline above will require considerable resources. While I would argue that such investment of resources would be justified, it is unlikely to happen very soon. It would be justified on the grounds that current, single-centred research – while giving us an excellent descriptive base, so that we now know what we need to explain, more or less, in terms of producing evidence-based policy, or even the evidence on which such policy could be based – has been almost totally ineffective, even after decades of investment in large-scale research projects. On that basis it must now be time to try something different, especially when it seems to hold out as much opportunity as game-theory research in education.

But even without large-scale investment, there is probably a good deal that could be done to build upon and systematize the kind of subjective data that I have alluded to when dealing with my own experience. Might we not take more seriously individuals' own accounts of how and why they arrived at various crucial decisions in their educational career? Could we not, through interviews and focus groups, try to understand why people leave school, and why they return to education later in their lives, if they do? And as a very positive starting-point, might it not be a good idea to stop asking what is wrong with them that made them drop out?

In this chapter I have tried to sketch out some of the possibilities and prospects held out by multicentred approaches to career-shaping choices, as a way of answering questions, and perhaps more importantly as a way of raising still more questions. I hope that this short outline has conveyed some of the excitement of those prospects.

Chapter 7

Equality of Opportunity

Equality of opportunity is an important feature of an educational system, and one which we expect to work towards, even if we are hesitant in claiming that we have actually achieved it. However, it is a slippery concept to grasp, as it is an emergent property of the system and not the property of any single person or event. Equality of opportunity implies a comparison of how different people fare in educational processes in comparison with others who come from similar backgrounds. On the other hand, the use of the term 'equality of opportunity' implies that we are not looking simply at equality of outcome, but that opportunity implies freedom to choose. So long as we frame the issues in terms of single-centred theories, it is difficult to imagine how we can address the issue of equality of opportunity without controlling and restricting individual freedom.

In order to illustrate these points more fully, and to make clearer the implications for education policy, let me go through one simple example at length. I say 'simple' because it is a single-policy area and involves only a limited aspect of education, but as will be seen, the implications are not particularly simple. The example that I have chosen is the recruitment of teachers by education authorities in the UK from developing countries such as South Africa.

The issue of 'brain-drains' is not new. That term was originally popularized in the 1960s and 1970s as a description of the flow of qualified researchers and professionals from the UK to the USA. But the basic issues arise in many educational contexts. The traditional apprenticeship schemes to educate craftspeople in the UK collapsed, to a large extent, because some companies found it easier to offer substantial incentives to attract newly qualified craftspeople from other firms than to train them themselves. This carries moral and political overtones, as do all other cases of brain-drain, in the sense that companies that are prepared to invest time, resources and effort in the future labour force are doubly penalized when companies that have not invested sweep up the best young craftspeople, and leave those companies that trained them without a skilled workforce.

And much the same considerations apply to the question of recruiting teachers from developing countries. Why should developing countries invest resources, effectively to subsidize an industrialized country that has not had the foresight or good grace to train its own labour force?

Before moving on, it is perhaps appropriate at this point to pause and note the models, frameworks or perspectives that we do not have available to us. We can relatively easily compare the salary of a teacher in London with that of a teacher in South Africa, and calculate that the migrant teacher could reckon their financial circumstances, in cash terms, very much improved by moving to London. We might make a more balanced calculation that took into account different costs of living, but still we would reckon that the financial rewards of teaching in London were better than those available in South Africa. Then, applying our single-centred economic models, we would expect individuals to follow the course of action that maximized their returns. That being the case, we would anticipate that the astute South African teachers would set off *en masse* for London, leaving the South African schools devoid of qualified teachers.

On the other hand, we may want to take into account the less tangible, non-financial rewards of working in London. We might want to compare the lot of a hard-working teacher scraping together enough money for the heating in a squalid bedsit in a poor London suburb, with rain running down ill-fitting windows on a February night while they do their marking under an electric lamp, thousands of miles away from relatives and friends, with that of the colleagues that they left behind. Surely, in the light of that equation, schools in South Africa need not fear any brain-drain.

If we think of the population of newly qualified teachers in South Africa as homogeneous, we can either think of them as all likely to migrate, or as none of them being willing to migrate. This is an example of the 'all-or-nothing' mentality that we have in relation to policy issues. This all-or-nothing view of policy arises directly from the single-centred nature of our models; if a homogeneous group of people faces a similar choice, and the calculation of benefits is straightforward and independent of all the other choices made, then there must be a 'right' answer that suits everybody, whether that is to go or to stay.

The situation is not much improved if we suggest that there is a sub-group of South African teachers who, because of their poverty or family circumstances, are more susceptible to economic exploitation by UK employers and willing to brave London in February. And talking about two homogeneous populations rather than one does not change the theoretical arguments at all.

So, having a propensity to imagine educational problems and issues in all-or-nothing terms, we also have a disposition towards educational policies or solutions that are all-or-nothing. We could put a stop to the recruitment of teachers in developing countries, by law, in either the UK or South Africa. We could make it illegal for UK public-sector employers to advertize and recruit in developing countries, or we could make it illegal for South African media to accept advertising from UK employers. Or, with more time and ingenuity, we could devise other mechanisms to put a stop to the drain on the resources of South Africa completely. But it is worth pondering the impact such Draconian measures might have upon the perfectly legitimate aspirations of South African teachers to improve their financial position. There are issues about the rights of individuals to move and to develop themselves which are important, and which are endangered by such complete imposition of state restrictions.

And if 'nothing' solutions do not appeal, then we can always let the matter be settled by market forces. Let everyone who wishes to move, or can be enticed to move, move, and the devil take the hindmost. Unregulated trade in goods and services is the only solution of those who do not care for the imposition of Draconian restrictions. In many ways it is not surprising that we set up situations where the opposing sides in the debate take up diametrically opposing positions, and then talk past each other.

The point recurs here that we do not have the frameworks to look at proportions of the population. Is there a level of movement which would be small enough to be acceptable to the South African educational system at the same time as being large enough to satisfy the desire of individuals to make their own decisions? Is there a level of movement, whether it is 0.5 per cent, 5 per cent or 50 per cent of the total population of teachers in South Africa, that could be lost in migration to the UK without doing substantial damage to either system or the individuals involved? And do we know what labour-market conditions, recruitment package or contractual terms would need to be offered in order to make 0.5 per cent of the teaching population move from South Africa to London, rather than 2 per cent or 5 per cent?

The answer is that we simply do not know the answers to any of these questions, and that is the point of the analysis offered here. The question (whether there is an acceptable level of migration) is couched in multi-centred terms. The policy question (of whether working conditions can be manipulated to produce acceptable levels of migration) requires a multi-centred approach. And the answers, if and when they come, will come from multicentred research. Single-centred research models cannot, and will not, address these policy issues.

There remains the question of the moral turpitude of the UK authorities in not having trained enough teachers for their schools in the first place. Is there anything at all that can be said about that? In spite of all evidence to the contrary, working out how many teachers are needed is not a very difficult task. Five-year-olds cannot be manufactured very quickly, and so the number of primary school teachers needed in the system can be known well before the training of new teachers needs to start. The lead times for recruiting secondary school teachers are even longer. Within the limits of accuracy of national census data, which is to say with a fairly high degree of accuracy, UK governments cannot be excused if they do not know how many children are going to be of school age. And from that it is a relatively small step to work out how many teachers are needed, and how many need to be trained. So why haven't they trained them and why do they have to recruit teachers from overseas?

The answer is that they have trained enough teachers, but for some unaccountable reason not all qualified teachers wish to work in our schools. Something in the pay, the working conditions, or the benefits of the training, leads many students to train as teachers but then not to become teachers. But the nation has trained enough teachers to staff our schools, if only all of those trained did as they are supposed to do.

I do not believe we can let the Department for Education and Skills off the hook quite so easily. In some subjects they have provided training places for every prospective teacher they can find, and they may not be culpable for a shortage of mathematics or physics teachers (in so far as recruitment onto training courses is concerned). But in many subject areas they could recruit more trainees if they chose to put the resources into the training programmes. And the phenomenon that many qualified teachers do not wish to teach is neither new nor unknown. So the fact that the UK authorities have trained enough teachers hardly gives them *carte blanche* to raid the labour-force of developing countries. They should have *overproduced* teachers to compensate for those who would not choose to follow their profession to the school gate. But should that have been an overproduction of 50 per cent, or 100 per cent or 200 per cent? If we have a homogeneous population of newly qualified teachers, what proportion of them would we expect to take up a career in school teaching? And do we know how to manipulate their working conditions, salary and prospects to change the percentage taking up such work in schools from, say, 80 to 90?

Again, we simply do not know. And so long as the Department for Education and Skills funds research that is designed to work out what is wrong with the qualified teachers who will not teach, we are unlikely to find out. That is to say, research into this topic has followed the now familiar line: if some newly qualified teachers teach, and some do not, then we must be looking at two, different, homogeneous populations, and all we need to do is work out which characteristic will allow us to distinguish between them. The research questions and policy issues are multicentred, the research that gets funded and dominates the literature is single-centred. And so long as this mismatch persists we will not be able to develop evidence-based policy.

We know, in a commonsense way, that all the key policy areas are multi-centred. Year after year, the staff who draw up timetables for schools calculate how many pupils are likely to want to study a particular subject, and allocate resources accordingly. There is the theoretical possibility that one year everyone will choose the same subject, but it is so remote a possibility that it is not worth taking into account as a planning assumption for a real institution. In the real world, for the purposes of developing policy and as a basis for developing scenarios for action, people develop a 'gut-feeling' about how many people are likely to make a particular choice.

In contrast with this very practical attitude, theoretical frameworks for examining policy tend to be single-centred, or all-or-nothing, in their perspective. Research examines why people differ, not how they will distribute themselves between the possible options. The result is that research and policy develop along parallel paths, without one informing the other. And this, naturally enough, leads to research, and theory, being undervalued by those with practical or policy concerns.

However, the danger of this separation of policy from theoretical research is more serious than that. Our common sense is indirectly shaped by theoretical research. At some level, single-centred research shapes our way of responding to the policy difficulties that relate to risk-management and the distribution of resources. Whenever we need to address issues of justice and fairness within the educational system, whether within a single country or, as in this case, in terms of the global system, we end up reverting to all-or-nothing thinking.

For example, when we have a number of young people living within an area, and we wish to allocate them to secondary schools, we can envisage two possible solutions. We can imagine a perfectly mechanical and bureaucratic way of allocating them, or we can imagine giving all parents a right to select the school their children attend. Of course, neither of these works. When there is no right to choose, some parents are disgruntled that their opinions have not been taken into account. But equally, parents cannot be given an absolute right to choose without very serious implications for resources.

These policy decisions then have a tendency to become simplified into a number of slogans, often with a little help from politicians. Consequently, at some deep level we know that public resources have to be rationed, unless we are all to struggle under the burden of tax, but we also know that 'postcode rationing' is wrong. The policy of inviting parents to express an opinion as to where their children should be schooled is simplified as a 'right to choose', even though no such right actually exists. We reject the idea of quotas and positive discrimination, even though we may not be clear about what exactly the impact of those measures would be.

In short, whenever we have to address issues of justice and fairness, our understanding of the system is such that our reasoning is incapacitated. Our thinking becomes dominated by the idea that the solution is so good that everybody will jump at the opportunity, and we are then surprised when they do not, or we are obsessed by visions of doom when we contemplate the possibility that everybody will do things that we do not want them to. Education is by no means the only area of public policy that is dominated by these boom-and-bust ways of framing issues. Parliament seems to be obsessed with legislating for every little misdemeanour and developing an immigration policy that is based upon the premise that everybody in Turkey (or Hong Kong, or wherever happens to be in the news at the time) may want to leave their homes behind and move to the UK. And this, apparently, rejoices in the name of 'the respect agenda'.

The core of this matter is the question of how to deal fairly with people within a framework of limited resources, at the same time as taking into account past unfairness. We recognize this as a difficult question, but appear to be addressing it through a completely strange, and in many ways ritualistic, response of apologizing for past events, without any sense of why a current office-holder should apologize for actions taken by their predecessors, or what difference this makes, or should make, to current policy.

At a personal level, many teachers have held the view that pupils who did not adopt the same values as their own were in some fundamental way mistaken. Pupils who did not value studying, or who dropped out of school, were not simply making a choice; they did not understand what was good for them. Advancing as far as possible in the education system was the best possible course of action, and those who chose to ignore this clearly did not understand their situation. It was perfectly reasonable for teachers to protect their egos in this way, because they were unlikely to run across the students who had made such a choice again, and overall the idea that teachers should have an ideological commitment to education probably did very little harm. However, we seem now to have entered into a period where all policy-makers and politicians have adopted a similar attitude. Politicians have good policies, but the public has not understood them.

An alternative policy framework is offered by market-based solutions. Markets are mechanisms for allocating resources, and at least have the merit of removing the need for resource allocation to be performed by policy-makers. (This comment relates to real markets, of course. Most supposed 'internal markets' or market systems in the public sector are not real markets at all because politicians, by and large, do not trust the public to make their own choices. As a result, such pseudo-markets as do exist are normally very heavily managed by policy-makers.) While markets therefore remove the need to allocate resources by policy fiat, and serve the function of matching supply to demand, they do not fully accord with our notions of justice and fairness. They cannot, for example, compensate for past injustices.

Moreover, there have always been goods which it has not been thought proper to distribute by market mechanisms. Votes, healthcare and the rights to life, liberty and the pursuit of happiness, are not now thought proper benefits to be bought and sold. Indeed, rights in general are seen to be too important to be purchased, or given in greater abundance to the wealthy, which is exactly why there needs to be a separate argument, namely that people have rights, to ensure that they are distributed fairly among the population. But the argument that people have rights does not resolve the difficulty, because where the multiple rights of different people come into conflict, rights cannot be held to be absolute and inalienable – which is their chief virtue. Resolving the conflicts between various rights of different citizens can only be achieved with a huge investment in litigation, as the case of the USA shows.

So we are left with issues of fairness and justice in education which are clearly related to patterns of overall distribution of benefits within the population, but where difficulties can only be resolved in relation to individual cases. A single parent or individual student may argue that they have been hard done by, that they have a right to choose their education, or indeed a right to education, but that case cannot be judged in isolation from the whole complex of what resources have been allocated to others.

And we are uncomfortable that market solutions will be used. We know, of course, that house prices may be higher near a very good school, since an address near the school may increase the likelihood of being allocated a place in the school. But we feel unhappy that the educational chances of young people should be settled by their parents' ability to pay inflated property prices.

Schools thrive when they have a small number of rebels and eccentrics. Nobody wants to see the Stepford Comprehensive School become standard across the country. But there is a difference between a school that cherishes 2 per cent of nonconformists, and a school that harbours 20 per cent of thugs and vandals. Good education involves giving everybody opportunities, knowing that only a few people will avail themselves.

But if we ask what the appropriate level of disobedience in a school is, we will not get a sensible answer. We will get an answer about zero-tolerance, and probably a lot of pious words about how this is achieved. What is an acceptable level of bullying in a school? One hardly dares to even ask the question. Every relationship carries within it the possibilities of domination, cruelty, excessive influence or some other feature which in excess might be undesirable. But in more moderate amounts, those same relationships might show leadership, discipline, persuasion and engagement. The only way to ensure that all relationships are totally safe is to stop them being real relationships at all.

Similarly, if we ask what circumstances distinguish between the case where 40 per cent of parents in a school want it to become a specialist city academy and the case where 60 per cent do, we have no idea at all. If we ask what structure of rewards and punishments encourage only 2 per cent of children to truant on any particular day rather than 5 per cent, we have no idea. Because research into overall distributions of people among the available choices have not been a focus of research.

Attempts to deal with perceived problems in the educational system have been shaped by all-or-nothing ways of framing those problems, with the result that generally zero-tolerance solutions have been advanced. Such solutions often raise difficulties which are just as severe, or even more severe, in their impact upon cherished civil liberties. If one wishes to stop truancy, is it a good idea to threaten parents with prison? Well, in fact, nobody knows, because nobody knows what are the appropriate incentives for reducing truancy. However, imprisoning parents seems to be a reasonable idea if one's goal is to reduce truancy to zero. If one's goal were to reduce truancy by half, a different approach might be more effective.

'What does not kill me makes me stronger': we are in some danger of trying to control our public systems of social interaction to the extent that any strengthening experiences are programmed out. Continual and relentless bullying cannot be condoned, but learning to deal with overbearing people is part of growing up. Children need to be protected from strangers who would do them harm, but there can be no substitute for them learning how to deal with the risks themselves.

For those of us who have survived our school years, it is probably a miracle that we did. Thinking back over all the possible bicycle accidents, road accidents, falls from high places that were narrowly averted, not to mention cuts and concussions, growing to adulthood is a risky business which cannot be totally controlled.

What theory should be doing is providing a better framework for talking about risk, about chances and opportunities, and about managing resources. To date, it has not been doing a very good job.

Anecdotal evidence

I have tried to illustrate the questions that relate to equality of opportunity within a range of settings that involve individual decisions and aspirations against a backdrop of mass decisions. These include the choices that an individual makes to apply for a place in an educational institution, a school or a university, to apply for work, or choose a career. In every case the setting in which such a decision is made is constructed not only by government and institutional policy but also by the aggregation of choices that other people make. Government policy may make it possible for me to apply for a place in a particular school, but it is the decisions of other people in the area that make the school popular or unpopular, and the competition for entry high or low.

And we routinely witness in the press the tip of an iceberg of concern that arises from these issues. An individual who appears to be well qualified is turned down by an educational institution. A much-vaunted government policy to involve local businesses in school governance does not attract as much interest as had been anticipated. Large investments in professional training and education fail to produce the required number of new entrants to the public services. And in every case the responses of politicians and the discussion in the press is simplistic because we do not have the appropriate frameworks to analyse and evaluate these questions of equality of opportunity. We know that we value the freedom of the individual to make an effort to improve his own situation, and we know that we do not wish people to be able to buy privilege by using their family's assets, either economic or cultural capital. But we do not know how to bring those two contrasting ideas into relationship.

And the only way we can confront such problems is complaining about the standards and measures used to distinguish between individual cases. The A level examinations do not differentiate adequately between the most able pupils, or the school admissions policy relies on measures that we do not deem important.

What all of these cases have in common is that there is a need to connect, in a conceptual way, the choices that individuals make with the behaviour of large groups of people. And this connection must work in both directions.

There must be a calculus that 'adds together' the behaviour of individuals to create a social environment, and we need a calculus that allows us to anticipate the impact of the social environment on individual choices. It is not that we do not have such frameworks: the problem is that our current, intuitive, understandings are too simple. They are single-centred. We think that a social environment will create a situation where there is one best choice for every individual in a homogeneous group. And, of course, we think that everyone will make that choice in a way that makes group behaviour unproblematic.

We have no theoretical frameworks that predict that a certain proportion of a homogeneous group will react in one way and the rest in another. So, although government and institutional policies frequently have targets, expressed in terms of proportions, these have no theoretical basis whatsoever. We know that we aim to have 50 per cent of young people experiencing higher education, but we have no way of knowing why 50 per cent is a better target than 40 per cent or 60 per cent. It looks achievable from present trends, and so we settle on that. Similarly, we know that we are concerned when more boys than girls (or more girls than boys) leave school without adequate qualifications, but we have no theoretical framework for assessing whether there is any reason why girls and boys should achieve in education in equal proportions, or whether the sex that is performing better is performing at the optimum level. We simply have some rather crude comparisons that lack theoretical justification.

All of which should make it clear that the direction of future research should be towards identifying theories that are multicentred, and address the shortcomings that present theories have. Some indications of where this should be done can be found in the current research literature.

Prior research

We have a very clear sense that we wish our education system to be fair. We frequently express this as a desire that there should be equality of opportunity for all. But as Cavanagh (2002) has noted, 'equality of opportunity' is a notion that is not particularly clear, sometimes being bound up with and confounded with simple egalitarianism or with meritocracy.

For example, when selecting applicants for university courses, it would be egalitarian to offer places at random, so that every applicant would have an equal chance of admission. It would be meritocratic to offer places to those with the highest scores on an admission test. Each of these captures an element of something that might be called equality of opportunity, but neither of them is satisfactory. Running a lottery to decide admissions to higher education would certainly mean that everybody (barring failures to register and other administrative difficulties) would have an equal chance of entering into a programme of study at that level. However, we recognize that for certain specializations at certain levels, prerequisites are necessary, and it does not offend our sense of fairness that there should be some restriction to entry on the basis of capability, previous knowledge and experience, or capacity to benefit. Our notion of fairness embraces treating different people in appropriately different ways, as well as treating equal people in equal ways. And that is perhaps why we use a phrase like 'equality of opportunity', rather than 'equality of outcome' or 'equal probability of success'.

On the other hand, a strictly meritocratic allocation of educational resources, with course places going to students on a strict basis of highest scores in an examination, runs into two kinds of difficulties. The first is the practical question of whether we can rely on our own abilities to measure performance with the degree of accuracy required. In countries where such a system is used, and there are many, the difference between outcome for two students may depend upon a difference in examination scores at the second decimal place, or a difference of as little as 0.01 per cent. Those who have been involved in any examination system and have a leaning towards the cynical may suggest that this is equivalent to running a lottery. But if a meritocracy is to be fair, then it must also be effective.

The second difficulty, which is really more serious, is that performance in educational tests depends upon prior learning and experience. It is not possible to set a university entrance examination which does not depend upon the prior educational experience of the candidate. In fact, it could hardly be desirable if it were possible, although I will return to that point shortly. So long as it is possible to prepare for an examination, performance in the examination must be skewed in favour of those who can command the best resources in that preparation.

One of the arguments for removing universal grants to support students through university that was advanced in the UK was that children from middle-class families were advantaged in the competition for places in higher education by virtue of their home background and access to better schools. ('Better schools' in this context might mean private schools supported by more resources, selective schools, or community schools supported by middle-class parents, but in any definition children from middle-class families had preferential access to them.) As a result, the wealthier segments of society were being helped disproportionately with their educational expenses in higher education. This has been resolved, as far as politicians are concerned, by first removing grants, and later by reinstating grants, but only on a means-tested basis so that the resources go to the less well-off. This simple example illustrates how complicated it is to identify the level of public support that should be given to students at different levels, and whether it is fair to have open competition for those resources.

There are certainly at least two approaches to overcoming this difficulty. The first is to look for a university entrance test which does not depend upon prior experience, but which in some culturally neutral way taps into the capability of the student. Something like an IQ test or scholastic aptitude test is advanced, which would measure directly how well the candidate was likely to learn, irrespective of his or her prior learning. The other is to ignore the question altogether, or at least to move it back to an earlier stage in the educational process; we cannot resolve the question of admissions to universities because experiences in secondary education are so variable. And doubtless we will very soon move the problem back further to the underlying inequalities in primary education and then in preschool.

As far as the quest for a culture-neutral, experience-neutral test of academic ability is concerned, it is, of course, the very worst kind of nonsense. IQ tests, and the like, have shown themselves to be very far from culturally neutral. It stands to reason that one's performance in any context will depend upon what one has learned previously, or at least that a test which could not be affected would necessarily exclude what Vygotsky referred to as higher mental functions, and would consequently be restricted to our functions as an animal, and therefore be irrelevant to selection for education.

The search for a content-free test that can select those most appropriately equipped for higher education is based upon a complete misconception of what the process of learning is all about. Dweck (2000) has suggested that people hold different self-theories, with some of us believing that intelligence is innate and others believing that intelligence can be developed through hard work and application. In Chapter 8, when I deal with issues of learning and teaching in greater depth, I will argue that the latter is the only tenable position to take within education. However, at this point it only needs to be noted that the search for a measure of ability unaffected by experience is clearly based in the idea that ability is innate, and one either has it or does not have it, and there is very little to be done about it.

Incidentally, Dweck describes interesting research on the question of how we should allocate scholarships to candidates applying for higher education. She demonstrates that those who favour the view that intelligence is innate would allocate resources to clever but idle candidates, while those who favour the alternative view of intelligence would allocate resources to those who work hard. This suggests that there may not be a clear and uniform answer to the question of what counts as 'fair' in education, and hence of what constitutes 'equality of opportunity'.

On the other hand, if we accept the idea that we cannot sort out equality of opportunity in higher education until we have first equalized opportunity in secondary education, and hence accepted the regress that implies, equality of opportunity is bound to remain a goal for the very distant future. Indeed, if we think about the question of what will constitute equality of opportunity at the moment of birth, we will need to ask the question of whether we need to equalize the wealth of parents so that they are equally able to invest in education of their children, and how we might take into account any mental capacities that are heritable. Policy dictates that if we wish to develop fairer education systems, we cannot afford to work systematically through the levels of education one after the other; we need more clarity about equality of opportunity at each level of education separately, and very quickly.

The concept of fairness in education, therefore, embraces not only the idea of treating people equally, but also of treating appropriate differences differently. What this brief foray into the issues around equality of opportunity indicates is that the concept is tied up with both the idea of everyone having some kind of equal probability of success, and the idea of assessing people's needs on the basis of merit, but not uniquely defined by either one of these contradictory principles.

To date, the problems that arise from this lack of clarity over equality of opportunity have not been developed further in the case of considering individuals. But in the related area of institutional evaluations there has been some concern over how to evaluate outcome measures (examination results) in terms of the social background of the institution concerned. This has largely been addressed through the concept of 'added value'.

Presumably a similar approach could be taken to the evaluation of individuals, looking at the improvement in performance over the immediately preceding cycle of education so as to compensate for inequalities in the earlier cycle(s) of education. Thus, if admission to higher education were to be based on value-added measures, a candidate would be able to demonstrate her ability to benefit from education by showing how much she has benefited from her recent education. Such an approach would produce something like a compromise between the strict demands of equality and meritocracy. However, as with all compromises, the risk is that an attempt to meet both criteria would result in neither being met.

The question of meritocracy is only partially met, because the point of educational qualifications (and this has become increasingly clear with recent redefinitions of standards) is to provide evidence that a clear criterion of performance has been passed. No matter how much improvement has been made in the recent cycle, if a candidate has not achieved a basic level of competence in performance she may still not be able to follow and benefit from more advanced study. On the other hand, the question of equality is put at risk whenever problems of measurement intervene and the possibility of error in the measures used, and consequently of treating equal performance unequally, arises. In the case of institutional comparison, Gorard (2006) has argued that the 'value-added' measures employed are so closely correlated with absolute measures of performance that they cannot, in fact, be measuring anything other than the outcome measures. In that sense, the use of supposed 'value-added' measures may give the illusion of correcting for past inequalities without making any substantial difference to the conclusions.

This indicates the general complication of this area, as to how the question of 'equality of opportunity' can be defined in a way that is practical, and can inform policy questions, and at the same time form the basis for research that can lead to the development of better policy. For there seems to be general consent that in some way, however that may be measured, the widening of access should lead to increased chances for the children of the working classes to attend successful schools, prestigious universities and generally achieve upward social mobility. Equally there seems to be surprise that the last three decades of widening access to university education has not had very much impact in this area. On the contrary, there appears to have been an increased strategic use of the public educational system by those with financial and cultural capital, using private education in the early cycles, and then returning their children to the state system to build upon the early advantage they have gained whenever there is no further benefit to be secured through putting in additional resources, or when it looks as though specific advantage may be given to those in state schools. Thus, gaining 'unfair' advantage, or at least securing special privilege, seems to be amenable to manipulation through specific tactics, while developing policy or even taking a general view on equality of educational opportunity at a general level seems to be quite beyond us. And this in spite of the fact that the government has set up bodies designed specifically to look into the question of equal opportunity to access in higher education.

At the core of previous approaches to equality of opportunity in education has been the assumption that differences in achievement must have definite causes in personal histories, and that those causes can be clearly identified through a process of research. In short, the idea of equality of opportunity has been underpinned by single-centredness, and the notion that there is one best route through the educational system. And behind that, there is the suggestion that there is a clear hierarchy of eventual outcomes, implicitly employment opportunities, rather than a multitude of different routes to a complex pattern of jobs and differentiated preferences for jobs. Of course, there is a possible solution here which would resolve the question, which is to say that each person has their own order of preferences, and that each individual must achieve the result that they wish, since if they were dissatisfied with the present result, they would invest more effort in achieving a different result. However, this is also too simplistic to provide an appropriate basis for policy.

However, a multicentred approach would certainly offer some opportunities to redefine, and therefore to open up for further empirical research, the question of equality of opportunity. The first question is to address how that might be done, and what it might mean for the debate on equality of opportunity.

A typical illustration of the difficulties over equality of opportunity arises when an individual case is highlighted in the media. This or that pupil of outstanding ability, as represented by excellent examination results, fails to gain entry to the university and course of their choice. The person in question comes from a group that has traditionally found entry to elite higher education difficult – they are female, from an ethnic minority or working-class family, or have attended a state school in a deprived area – and this is taken to be an indication of persisting lack of fairness in the system, and used to demonstrate lack of equality of opportunity.

The admission tutors of the course in question are hounded by reporters, and defend themselves by arguing that they have too many applicants with equally good qualifications, and they have not been able to offer places to all the well-qualified applicants. Moreover, they would love to be able to enrich their intake by recruiting more young people from inner-city schools, or working-class families, but they are unable to do so because those groups do not apply for the course in sufficient numbers. And in any case, they are hampered by the fact that the A level examinations do not allow them to pick out the very best applicants because too many applicants have the top grades.

This last point is an aside from the main argument that is being presented here, but it does need to be dealt with. A level grades are, and always have been, one of the worst predictors of success on degree programmes that we have available to us. There is no evidence whatsoever that if the grades at A level were more finely graduated, if it were possible to select only those who scored the very highest marks, that A levels would suddenly become a good indicator of likely success on an undergraduate course. In that sense at least, the linking of examination reform to equality of opportunity is a poor one. There may be other reasons for changing the system of examinations at the end of secondary school. We may wish to insist that young people demonstrate a broader range of knowledge and capability. We may wish course-work to be more or less heavily weighted in relation to traditional examinations. But the convenience of admission tutors in universities is not a sound principle on which to arrange the last two years of free, state-provided education.

The first point to note is that we cannot know from a single case whether there is a lack of equality of educational opportunity here or not. If equality of opportunity were only about selecting those with the highest marks for the most popular courses we could perhaps tell something from a single case. That would certainly make things simpler but would effectively remove the interesting aspects of the notion of the concept 'equality of opportunity', because it would make it impossible to take into account applicants who had worked hard and done well in spite of difficulties in their earlier schooling.

At this point, I want to take advantage of the time and effort that I and the reader have invested in the examination of multicentred models, and suggest simply that there are two multicentred phenomena that may be going on here. The first is that applicants are playing a game against Nature; a two-person zero-sum game with limited information. That case is relatively straightforward, as choosing a course of higher education is a career choice, and therefore the considerations set out in Chapter 6 apply to this case also. The other phenomenon is that applicants are playing a multiperson mixed-motive game similar to that set out as a model for class-room management in Chapter 5. Applicants have to choose between, for the sake of simplicity, an ancient university, a redbrick university, or a post-1992 university. The sum total of those choices shapes the character and ethos of the student body in each of those institutions, and hence shapes the nature of the student experience. In terms of the game-theory model, what all of the cohort of applicants choose helps to shape the benefits that are available from any particular choice.

As ever, I am not suggesting here that I have the definitive answer to all of these questions. What I am suggesting is that framing university choice as a game against Nature or a multiperson prisoner's dilemma does allow one to develop a sophisticated and sympathetic model of the decisions that real applicants face.

I hope, at the very least, that anybody who had read this chapter would not be tempted to argue that a well-qualified applicant who is turned down for the course of their choice is automatically an example of lack of equality of educational opportunity. Equally, I hope that nobody who has read this chapter would be tempted to argue that applicants who chose to go to a former polytechnic were foolish. In that sense, I hope that this chapter gives a more realistic view of what is involved in this complex area than we might get, say, from senior politicians. If this chapter does no more than move the debate, and associated research, a little in that more subtle direction, it may have achieved a great deal.

Future directions for research

The simplest way of characterizing the conclusions that arise from this chapter is that there is a need for research that looks at multicentred models. This can be captured very simply by stating that research questions should be framed in terms of a proportion of a population that makes a specific choice. Can we construct models of those choices that explain why 75 per cent of young people are motivated to achieve, but 25 per cent are not? Can we find changes in the circumstances that would shift that percentage to 80? In developing this model, can we treat the whole population together, or do we need to construct separate models for the two sexes? Or for different social classes? And if so, how many?

Even simply setting out the research questions in that format serves to underline what we have not, to date, achieved in educational research. We have been asking all-or-nothing questions and giving ourselves all-or-nothing answers. We will not be able to understand what we intend with our high-flying aspirations of equality of opportunity until we understand better why competition is so intense for some options and why some social groups think that the competition is not worth the candle.

Chapter 8

Learning and Teaching

In this chapter I turn my attention to an area that has been the focus of a great deal of educational research, namely the question of how and why people learn. However, the bulk of that research has focused upon the circumstances in which people learn, or the precursors of learning. Do people learn better in small groups or large? Do people learn best with individualized tuition? Is reading best taught through phonics or look-and-say?

In short, the question of learning is generally viewed simply as one of communication: has the message been transmitted well? Has it been received well? In developing the ideas set out in this chapter, I rely heavily on the work of Vygotsky. I trust that some of the parallels between the overall argument of this book and the arguments of Vygotsky will become very clear. Perhaps most importantly, I have commented that the imagination of educational researchers seems to be focused upon, or limited to, simple causal relationships, or single-centred models of human behaviour. Vygotsky makes a rather similar observation on the state of development of the field of psychology as he found it, and argues that psychology has only one mode for describing mental processes, namely stimulus-response:

> All psychological methods used at the present time in experimental studies, regardless of the great variety, are constructed according to one scheme: stimulus-response. No matter how unique and complex the type of setting of a psychological experiment might be, this universal basis can always be found in it. (Rieber 1997: 28)

Vygotsky looks at specific examples, both from behaviourism and from psychoanalysis, where the purpose is to understand complex, higher mental functions in terms of simple, atomistic and lower mental functions, whether those lower functions are simple reflexes or the sublimation of animal drives. In this monotone or single register of theoretical framing, Vygotsky finds the source of the inability of developmental psychology to apprehend cultural and social learning, or learning with a cultural content.

Vygotsky exemplifies this in the case of speech, where speech is regarded as a potential stimulus to activity in a physical or physiological sense, but the content or meaning of speech is excluded from the understanding.

> But in its [psychology's] own plan, it placed all sensory stimuli, including the human word, at the same level. In this sense, it factually coincided with physiology in its approach to higher behaviour of man. The one and the other were united by the methodological S-R pattern. In essence, the pattern forced experimental psychology, in the words of Binet, to equate the word with the ordinary sensory stimulus. It was necessary to reject the pattern, to disrupt it, or to subject everything to it. (Rieber 1997: 37)

Vygotsky's work, therefore, can be seen as an attempt to disrupt what he saw as the reductionist tendency of psychology and to create the space within which higher mental functions could be studied and described, taking into account the richness of the cultural content of those mental functions.

On the other hand, Vygotsky was a student of Pavlov, and consequently was himself attached to the scheme of stimulus-response, and saw in that scheme the prime operation of rudimentary or lower mental functions. So we need to examine his ideas relating to mental functions in general to see how he proposed to create the arena for understanding higher mental functions. How can Vygotsky use an understanding of stimulus-response to escape from purely mechanical – or in his terms physiological – explanations and create room for the emergence of higher mental functions of self-monitoring and self-control?

The child is born with certain animal responses, the ability or necessity to respond to certain stimuli in particular ways. For example, loud noises will startle a young child and draw his or her attention immediately. But, as Pavlov had shown, the response can be transferred to a conditioned stimulus by repetition, as when the mother first calls the child's attention by the (relative) loudness of her voice, but later the quality and tone of voice, or even the speaking of the name of the child, is enough to attract his or her attention. By progressive stages stimuli of greater and greater cultural content, and less and less directly linked to a loud noise, can be used to direct the child's attention. A bright red sign, a written instruction, even an exclamation mark can eventually be used to focus the individual's attention.

At some point in this process the child will recognize that he can substitute his own stimuli and give them specific meaning in relation to the response, and can therefore control his own behaviour. Rather than giving his attention to whatever happens to be making the loudest noise, the child learns to focus on the activity that produces the results he desires. Rather than relying on a shopping-list of chores that has been provided for him, he learns to write his own list of things to be done. By a process of successive reconditioning of responses, eventually a qualitative change is produced, which enables the individual to create his own stimuli – to direct attention, to remember, to produce original speech, etc. This process, which Vygotsky describes as 'mastery', takes place only with the higher mental functions, and provides a conceptual framework in which individuals can escape from the necessity of stimulus-response and can instead develop voluntary mental functions. The individuals can use the laws that govern lower mental functions in order to transcend them, and create a form of mental activity that is qualitatively different and cannot be reduced to pure stimulus-response in its rudimentary form.

I have written elsewhere, in a slightly different context, of obeying the laws of gravity while at the same time struggling to overcome them (Turner 2004a: 24). It seems to me that Vygotsky is describing a parallel process where the individual escapes the necessity of physiological re-action by using the very laws that govern those reactions.

I noted above that Vygotsky creates a theoretical space for 'the emergence of higher mental functions'. The choice of the word 'emergence' was not accidental. In complex systems, patterns at higher levels of systematic organization appear, which are not limited to, or fully described as, the sum of patterns at lower levels of aggregation. The description of molecules cannot be fully exhausted as the sum of the description of atoms, and the behaviour of biological systems is not merely the sum of chemical reactions. These properties are emergent properties of the complex system. In Vygotsky's schema, higher mental functions cannot be reduced to an accumulation of rudimentary functions, but are an emergent property of a person who is taking control of his own rudimentary capacities to transcend them.

Although the mathematical tools and analogies of chaos theory were not available to Vygotsky, it seems that he was striving towards something that might have represented an individual as a complex whole, using cultural tools to develop higher mental functions. In Vygotsky's vision of higher mental functions, a system of simple rules operating within a context of multiple feedback-loops and non-linear responses creates a situation where an unpredictable variety of personal histories can be generated.

Vygotsky still focuses upon the development of the child rather than the adult, even when his subject is 'higher' mental functions. It may be that this is because, as he notes of developmental psychology, it has been most successful dealing with the mental functions that are closest to the rudimentary and physiological, because the tendency has been to understand the higher functions by reducing them to their rudimentary components. In studying the development of higher mental functions, therefore, he focuses mainly on the acquisition, or genesis, of those functions in their early stages. While this is perfectly consistent with his view that what is needed is a history, a study of the functions in motion, it will leave (as will be seen) a good deal of space for speculation about the development of higher mental functions, and the role of education, and particularly education for adults.

The crucial discovery of Vygotsky's developmental history is that higher mental functions appear first in the public, social space, and only later are they internalized as personal and private knowledge. Children first learn to count using objects, counters or their own fingers, and only later develop the skill of counting silently 'to themselves'. Children first learn that reading is possible by hearing adults read from books, then later learn to read out loud, and only then, and finally, learn to read silently to themselves for pleasure or edification.

> We can formulate a general genetic law of cultural development as follows: every function in the cultural development of the child appears on the stage twice, in two planes, first the social, then the psychological, first between people as an intermental category, then within the child as a intramental category. This pertains equally to voluntary attention, to logical memory, to the formation of concepts, and the development of will. (Rieber 1997: 106)

From what has been said so far, the meaning of this should be very clear, although it may need to be emphasized that Vygotsky uses the word 'genetic' to indicate a general law covering the genesis of cultural development, rather than anything genetic as that would be understood in relation to genes and inheritance in the modern idiom. What is absolutely clear is the need to experience new concepts and skills represented in higher mental functions within a social and cultural setting, before they can become available for the individual to internalize. While Vygotsky stresses the universality of the law that he proposes in terms of attention, memory, concepts and the will, we might wish to extend that list further into the higher mental functions by adding reflection, professional judgement, the construction of justifications and arguments, the sifting and selection of relevant data and evidence, and many other areas that are of central concern throughout education.

This formulation of the development of higher mental functions as first 'intermental' and subsequently 'intramental' dissolves a number of difficulties. In the first place, it dissolves the problem of how an individual has concepts or mental categories that match her cultural world. This is not an accident or a coincidence, but a natural outcome of the learning process; the individual adopts the concepts and mental categories which are current in the culture in which she lives. There is no need for Platonism to resolve the question of how the structure of thought matches the structure of the world. But perhaps more importantly from the point of view of education, it clarifies what the teacher can and cannot do, and therefore what the teacher should and should not attempt to do.

The teacher can and should manage and manipulate the intermental sequence, and should structure this experience in such a way as to maximize the opportunities for the learner to engage with the concepts that are being used. As far as the intramental phase is concerned, the teacher can do nothing, apart from providing motivation, in the form of experiences which make the concepts under consideration important *to the child*. The skill and art of the teacher, therefore, rests in being able to provide social experiences that allow the learners to develop higher mental functions, and in explaining why and how those functions can be relevant to the needs of the learner.

One can frequently find complaints from colleagues that students will only pay attention to tasks that are assessed, with the implied criticism that this indicates shallowness or instrumentality on the part of the learners concerned. It is often represented as learning that is done in the wrong way, or in conflict with the spirit of the educational process. However, this is not at all a correct interpretation of what is happening. Rather, it is a job half done. The teacher, through explicit assessment and clarity of the criteria for assessment can manage the intermental processes, and direct the student's attention to particular aspects of the learning process. Neither the teacher nor the learner should forget, however, that the point and purpose of the learning exercise is not that the student should be assessed in the intermental space, but that she should have available to her the criteria, standards and values of the teacher for internalization should she find them valuable. In this subsequent process of internalization is the hope that the student will move from being a learner to being a reflective and self-monitoring professional agent. This gives a very specific meaning to the idea that through learning the student becomes a member of a community of practice. By adopting certain standards of behaviour and judgement, the learner transcends the need for a teacher, at least in so far as it relates to the specific things that she has learned.

In this sense, a student who will only concentrate on tasks that are assessed or carry credit is not a student who has gone off along the wrong path, but a student who is halfway along the right path.

Vygotsky says that:

> In general, we could say that the relations between higher mental functions were at one time real relations between people. I relate to myself in the same way that people relate to me. As verbal thinking represents an internalization of speech, as reflection is an internalization of argument, precisely so the mental function of the word, according to Janet, cannot be explained in any other way unless we bring into the explanation a system broader than man himself. (Rieber 1997: 103)

The skill and art of teaching as a profession lies in the creation of an educational environment that is filled with social relationships that will support the higher mental functions that we wish individual learners to develop. A great many conclusions may follow from this, not least among which is the certainty that critical reflection and questioning cannot be imposed by teacher on pupil via the application of authoritarian control or the mechanical specification of a classroom regime.

The extent to which we may have misconceived the whole educational process can perhaps be illustrated by examining one of Vygotsky's examples more closely. He was interested in studying higher mental functions by studying their genesis and development. Vygotsky looked in considerable detail at the development of memory, and in particular at the development of two forms of memory which he terms 'mnemonic' and 'mnemotechnical'. Perhaps rather confusingly, 'mnemonic' means that faculty of memory which is direct and purely physical, while 'mnemotechnical' means the operation of memory that is supported by the use of techniques that are cultural, such as the linking of an object to be remembered to a story or image (and, where the confusion arises, including mnemonics).

Vygotsky conducted experiments with young children to study the development of mnemonic and mnemotechnical memory. In experiments designed to test the memory of subjects using mnemonic or mnemotechnical means, he measured the number of items remembered correctly. A co-efficient was then calculated, indicating the percentage of items that were accurately remembered in a group set. In the preschool period, both co-efficients have similar values; a preschool child is not assisted by the use of cultural artefacts, such as prompt-cards, that can be linked to the objects to be remembered, and if the use of such cards is suggested to the child, their presence is as likely to confuse as to aid memory.

As the child grows, mnemonic memory increases slowly, or possibly not at all, while mnemotechnical memory increases rapidly. The curves representing the coefficients therefore diverge rapidly, with the coefficient of mnemotechnical memory rising more rapidly. Subsequently, the improvement in mnemotechnical memory slows down, and the coefficient may even remain static, while there is a rapid improvement in direct, or mnemonic, memory. Vygotsky describes the shape traced by the two coefficients over time as 'the parallelogram of the development of memory'.

Vygotsky offers an explanation of this shape in terms of what is known about the development of memory. The initial rise in the development of mnemotechnical memory is relatively easy to account for, as the child learns to use cultural symbols (prompt-cards) to supplement her direct memory. Subsequently, the child is able to internalize the processes that were once cultural, and to gain control over her own memory. As a result, the mnemonic function improves rapidly. Vygotsky states:

> We are inclined to think that there is a kind of revolution of mnemotechnical devices for remembering, that the child turned from external to an internal use of a sign and that in this way, direct remembering actually became mnemotechnical remembering, but based only on internal signs. (Rieber 1997: 186)

Vygotsky argues that the final feature, the slowing-down of the increase in the mnemotechnical function, is a function of the experimental setting in which the data was collected. The tests comprised fairly limited amounts of material to be remembered, and once this task was being performed well, there was not much scope for further improvement:

> To a significant degree, this explains the fact that the curve of mnemotechnical memory exhibits continuous deceleration in rate of increase. However, if we were to present more material for memorising consisting of several dozen or even hundreds of words, we would easily see, as our subsequent experiments will show, that the curve would exhibit a sharp upward trend. (Rieber 1997: 186)

At one level this is both extraordinary and unsurprising. If we imagine an individual learner, who studies material that becomes increasingly complex and demanding, then we might, according to Vygotsky's account, expect continuous improvement of both mnemotechnical memory and mnemonic memory, as the learner masters her own ability to manage her own memory, using first external symbols to order the cultural memory, and later using increasingly sophisticated techniques to organize the internal memory. First using simple memory structures, such as multiplication tables, chants and rhymes, the learner continues to internalize ever more complicated general principles, taxonomies and theoretical frameworks, to incorporate growing amounts of factual data. And always, the amount of memory that can be handled with the support of prompt-cards, reference books and directories is growing in such a way as to exceed that which can be held in active and direct memory. That which is available to direct memory eventually becomes little more than the 'key' to all of the memory that has been stored over generations as the accumulation of culture.

This is unsurprising in the sense that we witness in the career trajectory of those who are successful in our educational system something very like this, managing first relatively small amounts of knowledge that can be recalled for examinations, but gradually incorporating ever more information within their field of specialization and developing a mental map of all of the key points within their field of endeavour, rather than recalling individual and separate facts relating to their studies.

On the other hand, it is extraordinary in two senses. First, if Vygotsky is correct, there is no natural upper limit to the amount of material that can be mastered using a combination of mnemonic and mnemotechnical memory (or by using mnemonic memory transformed through the incorporation of mnemotechnical methods). The ultimate goal of education – or of the development of higher mental functions – might therefore be seen as the incorporation of all cultural knowledge into the learner's memory. The distinction is blurred between what is personal memory, in the sense that I can recall it immediately, and that which is cultural memory, in the sense that it is held in books in libraries. This blurring occurs because in the process of mastering my own memory, I have to incorporate cultural tools into my own memory, to revolutionize it to the point where 'pure' mnemonic memory is of little significance (although it may, of course, persist, as noted above).

There is an interesting parallel here with Popper's notion of 'third-world knowledge' or 'objective knowledge', namely that which is knowledge by virtue of it having been published, exposed to criticism, subjected to testing (and surviving those tests) and being available publicly or interpersonally. There is also a sense in which this contradicts Popper's view, as Popper, focusing on the generation of new knowledge, is interested in the process by which internal hunches, insights and guesses can be turned into objective, interpersonal knowledge. Vygotsky, on the other hand, is interested in the opposite process, whereby pre-existing culture can be made available, and subsequently internalized, by the naïve learner.

Finally, and perhaps most challengingly, Vygotsky's account of the development of memory is extraordinary because it should make us question the whole foundation of education. Education is not, cannot be, the process by which items are put into the memory of the learner for later recall. That would be an extremely limited, and largely pointless, activity, since it would stretch only the mnemonic memory, without providing the learner with the tools to master their own memory effectively. Mastering one's own memory necessarily involves mastering external, social and mnemotechnical operations which isolated learners drilling for examinations cannot be expected to come to terms with.

At the same time, while the use of external prompts to memory is a crucial part of the process of learning, education cannot be a process whereby the individual learns how to use a library catalogue. Unless the learner has internalized certain aspects of mnemotechnical memory, and has transformed and mastered his own memory, a library catalogue will be as useless to him as it is to a five-year-old child. Knowing that everything is known and out there somewhere in books is the same as not knowing it at all.

In the light of current contemporary debates about education, it is worth noting here that education cannot *only* be learning how to learn, or learning certain study skills. Education may involve learning those techniques, but must ultimately be about the learner mastering his own higher mental functions, directing attention, remembering, analysing, proving, reflecting, by internalizing cultural signs and tools so as to transform himself. Within Vygotsky's work we have a hint as to what the proper function of the teacher should be, and it is not to transmit inert knowledge of her subject.

Education is primarily about giving children and young people the social experience on which they can later base their own learning. Education, and educators, cannot control the intramental process of internalizing learning, but can aim to make the intermental processes as fruitful and as supportive of learning as possible. This ought to have very profound implications for the way that we think about classroom practice. As Vygotsky noted:

> Formerly, it was assumed that the function exists in the individual in a ready, semi-ready, or rudimentary form and in the group it unfolds, becomes complex, advances, is enriched, or, conversely, is inhibited, suppressed, etc. At present, we have a basis for assuming that in relation to higher mental functions, the matter must be presented as being quite the opposite. Functions initially are formed in the group in the form of relations of the children, then they become mental functions of the individual. Specifically, formerly it was thought that every child was capable of reflection, reaching conclusions, proving, finding bases for whatever position. From the collision of such reflections, argument was generated. But the matter is actually something else. Studies show that reflection is

generated from argument. The study of all other mental functions brings us to the same conclusion. (Rieber 1997: 107)

The job of the teacher, therefore, is to provide space for the 'collision of reflections' that will eventually give rise to the ability to reflect, to form conclusions and to establish bases for knowledge.

This has profound implications for what happens in the classroom, and for how we research what happens in the classroom. For example, previous research into the question of the impact of class size on educational outcomes has been of the straightforward causal kind: are the outcomes of learning (the amount of learning that can be repeated in a test) more or less in smaller classes? In contrast with that purely empirical position, we would expect the quality of education to be improved in smaller classes, because the opportunities for taking an active part in the clashes of opinion and collision of reflections will be much greater in small groups than in large. But now, drawing upon Vygotsky, the focus of study would be on how the individual used language and other cultural tools in those clashes, and what encouraged learners to internalize more of the learning available to them.

Similarly, rather than focusing on what the teacher does, whether they teach to the whole class or to differentiated groups, the focus of research would be on what the learners do: how do they interact, and which kinds of interaction are particularly fruitful?

This is not entirely new, either in terms of pedagogic practice or research procedures, as learning has always gone on in classrooms and students have always interacted, often in spite of the activity of teachers. Similarly, classroom researchers have often focused their attention on what learners do, but without a theoretical framework such observation has tended to be extremely limited. For example, research has focused on the time that learners have spent on-task. But this is entirely analogous to the example cited by Vygotsky in relation to the spoken word. The spoken word is not simply a physiological event like any other stimulus; it has cultural content. And similarly time-on-task is not all the same, but in reflecting upon it one needs to take into account the cultural content of the task to which time is being devoted.

In this way, research into constructivist approaches to learning is given a new twist. Constructivism, as I have presented it here, is no longer simply about activity on the part of the learner. It is about specific kinds of activity in relation to language and other cultural tools, and it needs to be understood in terms of the relationship between the intermental and intramental phases of learning.

Anecdotal evidence

It is not really surprising that this question of what constitutes a sound basis for learning and teaching has been at the forefront of the thoughts of educational reformers over the course of centuries. And yet, at the beginning of the twenty-first century, we seem to have very little in the way of consensus about how education should actually be conducted. There are still debates over whether we should teach reading as a system of symbol recognition (phonics) or whether we should concentrate on some larger and broader sense of communication – what reading is about.

We might note, for example, that Rudolf Steiner argued for the latter position; until a child understands what reading is for, where it fits into social interactions and how it will make his life more rewarding, we cannot expect him to devote the amount of effort to the task of mastery that is necessary to make a fluent reader. For Steiner, play was the means by which a child learned about his place in the adult world. Playing with a toy post office – putting messages in envelopes, franking them and playing at their distribution – gives children an insight into the role of written language in communicating with those who are distant. Reading stories to children from books gives them an insight into the notion that one might read a book for pleasure. Through play and pleasure a child can learn what the overall purpose of the task is, and why he might put himself to the trouble of learning it. But for motivational purposes, the child needs to see the big picture first.

In contrast with this, Maria Montessori argued that we should not wish to engage the reason of the child at this early stage, but should prefer to engage their senses. Thus by providing children with sensual material, such as letters made of textured materials that they can run their fingers over, they may become familiar with the shapes of letters before needing to know what they are for. In this way the senses can be developed, and children can learn what we would now call prereading skills before they have any idea that there is such a thing as reading as understood by adults.

In one form or another, this debate has been at the heart of educational theorizing for the last 200 years: are teachers imparting skills, in the sense of discrete, atomic abilities, or are they giving children a vision of the whole sphere of understanding to which they are being introduced? Put that starkly, the obvious answer is that both are required, and that would make sense to any teacher. But the fact remains that we do not have a framework of understanding that allows us to bring the two perspectives, the macroscopic overview and the microscopic training, together in an overall picture. What I am arguing is that Vygotsky gives us such a framework.

In the intermental sphere, the teacher can provide structure and drill in specific skills. But in order to make it possible for the learner to incorporate such skills into their own mental repertoire, to be successful in the intramental sphere, the teacher must also provide a broader understanding of where such skills fit in, so that the learner is motivated and able to fit them into the body of knowledge that she has already accumulated.

Of course, I am not arguing that Vygotsky is alone in offering a framework for understanding learning and teaching. George Herbert Mead, for one, offers a similar framework. And it is interesting to note points of similarity between the lines of argument that are adopted by Vygotsky and Mead. Mead describes himself as a 'social behaviourist', which is an interesting turn of phrase, because it highlights the physical basis of mental functions – which parallels Vygotsky's insistence that mental functions grow from conditioned responses – at the same time as stressing the social nature of knowledge and learning (Mead 1967: 1–41).

Mead goes further in stressing the links between social interaction and learning, stating that in order to use a skill effectively it is frequently necessary to be able to see one's own situation from the perspective of others. He uses the example of games, where it is not enough to have a specific skill – the ability to wield a baseball bat effectively. In order to be a good player, one needs to know how batting fits into the purpose of the game and the goals of one's own side. But, and this is crucial, one also needs to understand the game from the perspective of one's opponents. Understanding the pitcher's goals and thought processes help one to apply the batting skill more effectively. Understanding what the fielders have to do helps the batsman to know where to place the ball to make their life as difficult as possible. In order to play one role in the game effectively, one has to understand what everybody else's role is, too (Mead 1967: 151–2).

This is not only true in sports, but is a consideration in the application of very many skills. Reading aloud is only partly a question of deciphering signs to make sounds; quite as much it is about empathizing with the person giving the message and placing stress upon the phrases in a way that is not indicated in the text at all, but arises from the understanding that this is a communicative process. The reader must also understand the roles of the writer and the listener. Speaking in public or making a presentation, clear diction and proper breathing do not do any harm, but projecting a message involves much more than skill: it requires an understanding of what the audience wants. In this sense all learning requires a sense of social empathy quite as much as it requires a memory.

The example of games is interesting, however, as it suggests that rule-governed games may have a function in the education of children which is of great importance, quite apart from anything that it may do in the way of physical exercise. This may certainly be an area that would merit further research, into whether games, and games of particular sorts, have a unique developmental function in the learning of that most important of social skills, the ability to see the situation through the eyes of others. There has been a good deal of research into the use of games, both simulations played in the classroom and games using computers, in the teaching of different aspects of the curriculum, but that research has not generally focused upon the role of games in helping young people to see things through the eyes of others.

Prior research

There has, of course, been a great deal of research on learning and teaching, both among young children and adults. But education studies are more prone to needless and sterile debate than most areas of human endeavour, so much of the research has been designed to show that people can be classified in this way or that, or that this style of teaching is more effective than that. Thus we have studies of learning styles that are designed to show that different people learn in different ways, rather than suggesting that each individual may employ many different ways to learn, depending upon the circumstances. Indeed, there is the slightest suggestion that learners who are in some way 'strategic' may be rather underhand and avoid the true purpose of education, which is to imbibe all knowledge in an undifferentiated way and with a happy heart.

After the debates about whether there are four learning styles or three, there is the research that suggests that there are no learning styles at all. And of course there is the research that shows there is a learning cycle, or even a double learning cycle, that in some ways parallels the 'social followed by internalization' description advanced by Vygotsky. Thus we have Schön's work on reflection and the role of the professional practitioner, and Argyris and Schön's work on double-loop learning. Such work points in an interesting way to the conclusion that there may be an overarching theory of learning and teaching that might be developed on the basis of the foundation laid by Vygotsky and Mead. But the fact of the matter is that no such firm basis has yet been set.

I think that there are two very good reasons why such a cumulative development of understanding has not taken place. The first is that educators still tend to place themselves at the ends of spectra in debates, and particularly to take up sides in favour of skills or in favour of an holistic overview. Hence, even such a global concept as 'professional reflection' tends to be interpreted as defining a skills base by those intent upon seeing the detailed picture, while those who want to see professionalism as an integrative art stretch the idea of reflection to the point where it offers little in the way of practical guidance.

The second obstacle to developing a clear understanding of learning is that many involved in educational research have a commitment to their base profession, namely teaching. Vygotsky therefore tends to be interpreted as a defence of teaching, rather than as a basis for learning. As I have noted, the important aspect of the intermental phase of learning is that it should be couched in terms of publicly accessible language, arguments and evidence presented in conformity with publicly available standards, and tested in a social context. But as Vygotsky himself noted, this can be done by an individual in isolation, who may speak to himself in the course of a task, using public signs to manage his own internal processes. Educationists, however, normally latch on to Vygotsky's description of learning as being supported by a teacher or more proficient peer (in my view simply an exemplification of some of the ways in which the learning can be social) to conclude that the learner needs to be 'taught'.

As a result, teachers figure very prominently in current interpretations of Vygotsky, and the Zone of Proximal Development (or ZPD) is the feature of his work that attracts most comment. Properly understood, the ZPD is the difference between what the learner is able to do with social signals and what the child is able to do on his own. The ZPD might be the difference between the account that a child gives on his own, compared with the account he gives when prompted and guided by a questioner who structures the questions in order to receive a logical and coherent narrative. But equally, the ZPD could be the difference between mnemonic memory and mnemonotechnical memory, the difference in understanding produced by social tools, so that integrating them into one's mental functions produces a change which is subsequently invisible. The ZPD is not, although it is often held to be, the difference between what a child can do alone and what a child can do with a teacher's support.

Since we are dealing with the arena of education studies, there is, of course, an entirely contrary perspective, derived from humanistic psychology, which suggests that a teacher cannot teach anything: each individual must learn what it is he chooses to learn. Again, this position is valuable, and its value can be seen in the context of Vygotsky's work. Nobody but the learner can manage the intramental phase of learning. But that is rather different from suggesting that people can only learn what they teach themselves. Without the intermental phase of learning, the learner does not have any knowledge that can be internalized. So, far from concluding that the teacher has no role, what we must conclude is that the teacher has a crucial role, but that role is strictly bounded and cannot substitute for the learner's own efforts.

Future directions for research

Future research in this area of education should be directed towards building up a comprehensive understanding of how people learn. Although many of the pieces of such research may be available, we need to see learning as a phased process, some of which is capable of being regulated, controlled and managed by teachers, and some of which is not capable of being controlled by anybody but the learner, but all of which needs to be understood.

That sounds very simple, but it would, of course, rule out much of what passes as research into teaching at the moment. Research which seeks to identify which teaching styles or methods of classroom management lead to the best learning outcomes is misguided. Learning outcomes cannot be controlled in such simplistic ways. However, understanding how teachers can increase the availability of knowledge for later internalization is of crucial importance to understanding how we could improve the professionalism of teachers as a whole.

Montessori's goal was to build a scientifically designed learning environment, in which the child would teach himself without the interference of adults. The line of argument presented here suggests that this may not be desirable, in the sense that learning starts as being social. But let us suppose that Montessori's goal was so to incorporate cultural signs and meanings into the classroom and its apparatus that the child would have his learning fully supported by cultural means; then we can at least see the merit of Montessori's method in removing from the child's environment all of those adults who wish to exert inappropriate control, to manage the child's thinking processes before he has learned to manage them for himself. I like to think that Montessori's goal was to remove that kind of control from the infant classroom that we have all seen, and which is so often demotivating, where adults have schedules and programmes that they expect the child to follow.

I think that we have to separate Montessori's goal of establishing a science of designing educational environments from the specific expression of that goal which is captured in what is now known as the 'Montessori method'. Her original goal of identifying what sort of equipment and classroom management made it possible for children to educate themselves, was, in my view, a very proper purpose for educational research, and perhaps the goal above all others towards which educational research should be directed. However, after an initial burst of insight and originality, that approach appears to have become frozen into a method that has not received much in the way of new science. And by becoming frozen, it has not been able to form the basis of the larger vision that Montessori offered us. That is something that we should strive to put right now.

On the other hand, there is much that we need to understand about how the learner's self-image helps or hinders in the processes of internalizing the knowledge that is put in front of him by teachers. Dweck's work is an example of what might be done is such a sphere.

Above everything else, Vygotsky's vision of education is that through a process of learning we come to be able to manage ourselves. Understanding what cultural signs and values are of most help in managing our own attention, memory and responses is central to the educational endeavour, and how we should think of ourselves and our learning processes to support that endeavour is an important area for educational research. And it may have benefits far beyond the classroom.

In suggesting a future direction for research that is based upon the work of Vygotsky I am suggesting an advance on two fronts. The first is that by looking at Vygotsky's work on learning as such we can find a model that is both meticulous in its attention to experimental detail and comprehensive in its approach to cultural issues. It provides a way of examining what young people actually do when they learn, but also leaves space for the meaning of what is learned. In that sense, Vygotsky is not just another psychologist of learning, to be mentioned in the same breath as Skinner, Piaget or Rogers. He is much more important than that, in the sense that he leaves space for the inclusion of culturally distinct learning, learning that has meaning. In that sense, I would argue, he is as simple as possible, but not simpler.

I have, however, mentioned Mead as a possible equivalent to Vygotsky, in terms of having a framework for understanding social knowledge that is sufficiently robust to frame the research and knowledge that we need to develop. In that sense, I am not suggesting that Vygostky is alone, but rather suggesting that it is time, after 400 years of reflecting on pedagogy, that educational researchers were able to bring together a view based on what we have learned. And, in my opinion, Vygotsky would be central to any distillation of 'what we know about education'.

But the second front on which Vygotsky urges us to advance is equally important. I have noted that in many ways Vygotsky seems to be struggling towards a concept of a person as a chaotic system, even though he did not have the language of chaos and complexity theory available to him. Learning is a process by which the individual increasingly develops feedback links from thoughts to conditioned responses, so that conditioned responses can be controlled by ever less significant stimuli. The process continues until the butterfly effect can be seen at work in our own responses and our own motivation. Of course, we do this with the intention of managing our own responses, but we cannot always control where we end up. I was made by nature to have a physiological response when confronted with a roaring lion: increased adrenalin in the blood, increased heart-rate, increased flow of blood to the muscles, and so on. I have gained mastery of my own responses to the point where my anger can be managed and controlled by cultural stimuli. But the price I pay for that is that very small stimuli, and not always the ones that I would choose, can call forth the same response. Five minutes into a telephone call with a call centre, trying to make contact with a living person, and my responses are every bit as physiological as if I were confronted by a lion. What we can see from this is that by careful development of mastery through the use of language we can manage our response to a real lion. But the responses that are physiological, and in the long-run may be very damaging, can also be stimulated by cultural experiences, such as stress in the workplace or fear of examinations.

And that means that Vygotsky has something to tell us, not only about our personal psychology but also about the institutions that we can inhabit, and in particular about the educational institutions in which we can learn. Those institutions must also be complex and capable of responding in complex ways. And they must leave space for the individuals within them to learn. (It is the fact that none of the options I am given by the call centre exactly correspond to my circumstance that reduces me to apoplexy – an assumption that there are five simple cases and everybody must fall into one of those five.)

Vygotsky's theory of learning therefore has important implications for how institutional change is managed. We know very well, because we hear it in connection with practically every process of institutional change which is mentioned, that those who are involved must 'own' the changes for themselves. Using Vygotsky, we can develop an understanding of what this might mean. Senior managers can explain the point and purpose of the change (the interpersonal), but each actor must have an opportunity to come to terms with the new processes, to decide where they fit alongside their old understanding of the world, to decide what they mean to them, possibly to decide to resist or adapt certain aspects, and so on (the intrapersonal). In this intrapersonal process, an innovation is not simply an innovation, it is a specific innovation with specific cultural meaning. Treating all innovation as generic innovation is on a par with treating speech as a physiological stimulus, as discussed above.

This highlights two other possible interpretations of what it might mean for participants to 'own' the change themselves. The first is that they have to work out what the change will be for themselves. In essence, this is a withdrawal from the interpersonal phase by those who supposedly lead the change. A teacher who is not committed to a particular outcome for her students, or at least a range of desired outcomes, seems either to lack the commitment necessary to be a teacher, or she is feigning an openness to outcomes while trying to manipulate her students into choosing the intended goals. It has, for example, always struck me as highly suspect that in Freire's method, cultural circles were expected to identify their own thematic words, and yet, mysteriously, these were always the same for all cultural circles. Either the facilitators were giving guidance, or the thematic concerns were the same in all settings. In Vygotsky's terms, giving guidance in the interpersonal stage was quite legitimate, but followers of Freire always denied such guidance was necessary. But the idea that all cultural circles produced the same thematic concerns was somehow unbelievable, and seemed to suppose that there was no real room for social differences in the method.

The other interpretation of what it means for the participants to 'own' the change for themselves is that the change is given by central policy, but the local participants need to be given time to accept it to adjust to it and possibly to be managed into it. This could be dressed up in terms that treat all changes as generic: 'Change raises anxiety and emotional responses, and we need to be able to manage the emotions of the participants.' I find this the most dangerous approach, because it presumes that the participants are not able to manage their own emotions, at the same time as it attempts to remove any cultural meaning or content from the process of change.

In contrast with these two interpretations, Vygotsky's approach provides a legitimate role for central leadership, while acknowledging the importance of the participants, and of the cultural value they attach to the content of the proposed change. In that sense, Vygotsky's theory of learning provides a framework for understanding and describing processes of institutional change in complex managerial systems.

Turning this around: if a structured approach to learning theory can inform policy processes and processes of institutional change, does this not suggest that learning theory is necessary to a proper understanding of those social processes? From my own perspective I would say that the answer was yes. I am becoming increasingly frustrated by conferences on education where paper after paper is presented, none of them addressing a theory of learning at all. Changes are introduced and explained on a market model (more local decision-making will lead to more effective decision-making) or a diffusion model (pilot or beacon schools will be established in each area, and the good practice will spread from there) or a bureaucratic model (policy directives will be issued from the ministry and implemented in the regions), but no attention is paid at all to how individuals within the system will learn about these initiatives, or how they will respond to the cultural meaning and content of the proposals. I think that Vygotsky at least gives an indication of how these important connections could be drawn.

Throughout this book I am trying to draw connections between different levels of educational activity, whether that is the kindergarten and the university, or the learning that goes on in the classroom or the learning goes on among policy-makers. In complex systems, patterns show a tendency to repeat themselves at different levels of aggregation (as in the Sierpinski Triangle described in Chapter 3). This is one of the reasons why a chapter on learning and teaching is included here, even though it would not normally find a place in a book which focuses principally on policy. I hope the result is as suggestive of future directions for educational research as is anything else in this book.

Chapter 9

Quality Assurance

We see a growing concern that education should be 'fit for purpose'. For example, the White Paper on further education (DfES 2006) uses the term on four occasions – in relation to the system as a whole and in relation to the qualifications framework. But the implications do not seem to be followed through effectively. In the first place, 'fit for purpose' as an expression raises the questions of 'which purpose?' and 'whose purpose?' It suggests the idea that the goals an educational institution might be oriented towards are multidimensional and contested, and implies the multicentred interpretation that there is not one best way for an educational institution to operate.

On 18 January 2006 the Select Committee on Education and Skills took evidence as to whether the statementing process was 'fit for purpose'. The chairman of the committee commented: 'Is that not at the heart of the problem? There is a sense in which there is no bog-standard child: every child has special educational needs at one level . . .' (House of Commons 2006). This is a recognition that the education system needs to be multicentred in order to accommodate the variety of learning needs that are presented.

And there is only one realistic way in which this can be achieved, and that is through the efforts of reflective, professional teachers who are equipped to respond to the diversity of needs and purposes that they confront. There is no way that teachers can be prepared, in preservice training, for the variety of demands they will meet in the course of their professional lives. They will need to be able to examine their own capabilities and the resources available in order to extend their practice to new areas. The teacher who has extensive experience of dealing with hearing-impaired children, for example, will not necessarily be able to transfer her practice to children who are visually impaired unless she is prepared to learn more about the specificities of those special learning needs. Above all the professional teacher will need the ability to use research, to incorporate the insights developed though research into practice, and to extend her understanding of her own practice through the application of research. In short, the teacher will need to be a researcher in order to support quality education throughout her career.

I think of myself as a researcher. I take pride in my research skills. But I want to stress that I do not see research as separate from ordinary life. As part of professional activity I think of research as the ability to pull together information that can form a useful foundation for action. Let me illustrate this with an example.

Some years ago my wife went to stay with a family with whom we have been friends for many years. Shortly after she arrived with them she rang me, not just to say that she had arrived safely but to say that our friend, whom I will call Eve, was extremely worried. Eve, who was pregnant at the time, had been to her doctor, and the doctor had conducted some blood-tests on her. The tests had shown that there were high levels of gamma globulin antibodies in Eve's blood. The doctor had told her not to worry, obviously with not much effect, and had also asked her to come back for further tests at a later date. Eve wanted to know more about what the tests indicated, why she had high levels of gamma globulin antibodies. To set Eve's mind at rest my wife asked me to find out what I could.

My first step was to go into the Internet and, using one of the major search engines (my personal preference is for Google), to look for websites that mentioned gamma globulin antibodies. As anyone can easily confirm, the result is that the search engine identifies some tens of thousands of websites which meet those criteria. This is, perhaps, an important point in terms of research skills. Finding information is very rarely the issue: it is more important to be able to sort, sift and classify the information that one finds in order to make it manageable. It is in this critical and evaluative process that the real research skills lie.

In order to start that sifting process, I began a process of reading through the first few websites which had been identified as relevant to the issue of raised levels of gamma globulin antibodies. I quickly came to realize that many, though by no means all, of the websites, referred to raised levels of gamma globulin antibodies during pregnancy. As a consequence of that information, I was able to narrow my search and reduce the number of irrelevant websites that I was looking at. The second realization that I came to was that much of the information, if not many of the actual expressions, was repeated from one website to another and that, in practice, there was very little disagreement about the explanations being offered. As a result of these developing insights, I could bring the information together concisely, and what I found out could be summarized as follows:

Raised levels of gamma globulin antibodies in the second or subsequent pregnancy can possibly indicate that the mother's body is treating her foetus as a foreign implant and is in the process of rejecting it. The high levels of antibodies are a result of the imperfect operation of the placenta in an earlier pregnancy and it suggests that the placenta is incapable of protecting the mother and the foetus from each other. The prognosis in this condition is, of course, very serious.

There are however other conditions which are indicated by high levels of gamma globulin antibodies. These include previous infections from colds or influenza in the preceding months. Such an infection may have been so mild as to produce no clinical symptoms, even though it led to raised levels of antibodies.

My conclusion after perusing the websites that I had available was that the tests indicating high levels of antibodies indicated one of two things: that Eve was experiencing some difficulty in her pregnancy which was extremely serious, or alternatively that she had had a cold some time in the previous six weeks and had nothing to worry about. I selected a single website that explained this information in the clearest possible format and made a note of its address to pass the information on to my wife and our friend.

If we look at my progress as a researcher so far in this case, we can see that I could have stopped as soon as I had found some information. I could have e-mailed my wife and said, 'If you go into Google and search for "gamma globulin antibodies", there are 20,000 sites with all of the information that you might need. Go and have a look!' But what I had actually done was to identify a typical site which had all of the information that I thought that she needed in the clearest possible format. I had selected a site on the basis of its clarity. I had also selected it on the basis that it came from a reliable source, in this case a university medical school in the United States. I had also satisfied myself by browsing quickly through a number of websites that there was a broad consensus of what the raised levels of antibodies indicated as part of a medical history. By exercising judgement over the quality and variety of information that I was identifying, I was able to pass a concise summary on to my wife.

I could easily recognize, however, that the conclusion that I had arrived at was not really a satisfactory answer to the original research question. The original research question, as I now understood it, was 'Am I or my baby at risk?' To that question, the answer that this condition is either very serious or of no consequence whatsoever is not a satisfactory answer. What I needed to know was the likelihood of the condition being serious. Could I say with any confidence to Eve, 'There really is not much to worry about'? For that I needed to find out under what circumstances the doctor would have prescribed the additional tests and what it was that the doctor was surmising.

Armed with that more closely formulated question I was able to refine my search and look for information about blood-tests, and their use during pregnancy, in cases where the patients showed raised levels of gamma glo-bulin antibodies. The result of this reformulated search was a much smaller number of sites with information that was quite specific. Relatively high in the list of websites returned by this new, narrower search I came across the advice to doctors from the American Medical Association (AMA). The AMA advice indicated the circumstances in which doctors should use addi-tional tests.

In my reading at that time (and of course the advice changes from time to time so I have no idea if the information is still current) the AMA described the circumstances in which a mother could be regarded as particularly at risk. Where a mother had suffered two previous miscarriages in a second or later pregnancy, the AMA advised doctors to test for higher-than-normal levels of gamma globulin antibodies and on finding them to prescribe addi-tional tests. To summarize this advice very briefly, two prior miscarriages indicated that the mother was at increased risk of rejecting the current baby, and the subsequent tests were to assess whether the raised levels of gamma globulin were associated with the pregnancy or with a previous mild infection. In the case that the antibodies were associated with the preg-nancy, and therefore showed higher levels of risk, they would go up in the subsequent test. In contrast to this, if the high levels of antibodies were the result of a previous cold, they would go down over the subsequent few weeks before the second test.

From this second website I was able to draw another important conclu-sion which helped to answer the original research question, namely that Eve's doctor was being more cautious than the advice of the AMA required. He had prescribed blood-tests even though Eve would not, on the AMA advice, be described as 'at risk', and he had done exactly what one would have hoped for, which was to prescribe a second set of tests in order to rule out a possibility that the antibodies were associated with a previous mild infection. I was able to conclude and therefore to pass on the information that Eve's doctor was treating her case with particular caution and was taking the steps which were offering Eve a greater protection that would have been provided by the advice of the AMA in such cases.

I had now reduced the vast amount of information that I have encoun-tered to two websites, both authoritative, one of which described the exact circumstances in which Eve now found herself while the second explained what her doctor was doing and how much confidence she should place in those actions. The results of that more focused search were, I thought, reas-suring. But it left open a further important research question which I felt needed to be answered before I could give a complete response. Had I been in Eve's position and received the information as sorted and sifted thus far, I would have been left with one major concern: supposing a second set of blood-tests showed raised levels of antibodies, would that be a disaster, or would there be some treatment or intervention which could be taken at that point? In other words, what happens if the worst comes to the worst?

Again, with that more specific and refined question in mind, I was able to conduct a search and identify an authoritative source of information, in this case again the website of a university medical school. This indicated that there were indeed courses of action that could be taken if the second set of blood-tests showed raised levels of antibodies, and that those courses of action were almost always successful.

So to summarize, I had been able to sift and sort through a wealth of information and reduce it to only three websites. In the course of that sifting I was confident that I had not lost any crucial information. I was able to provide general information about a medical condition to Eve. I was also able to explain what her doctor was thinking the risks were and why she had chosen to prescribe additional tests. Finally I was able to indicate that there was probably nothing to worry about, but that even if there was, there were still courses of action that could be taken. I thought that probably covered all of the immediate questions that I had been asked to address, however vaguely, in the first instance and that I could pass that information on with confidence to my wife and friend.

In this illustrative case what I think I have shown is that the research skills which are being employed are much more than simply identifying sources of information. The important elements include a mapping of the background information and of what is known about the area in general. In particular, the researcher is attempting to map what I would describe as the topography of the area of knowledge. Is there a consensus on the main points under discussion or are there sharply competing camps? If there are sharply competing camps, what are the main questions which divide them and are they matters of basic philosophy or epistemology, or are they matters of purported fact? And where there are distinct differences between competing views is there any obvious explanation for such differences? These might include changes over time, or changes to reflect more recent evidence, or an association of one view with a particular philosophical position or position in society. In arriving at all such conclusions, the researcher is constantly weighing the authority or experience of the person who provides the information and the confidence which can be placed in their judgements.

In the particular example discussed here, there was in fact a consensus of assorted information identified and consequently there was less need to identify sources which could be regarded as particularly authoritative. However, my search did identify sources which I regarded as authoritative and the provenance of the evidence – from an established, national professional body, or from a publicly funded university – added to my confidence that I was not relying on the views of witnesses who were partisan or particularly eccentric. In addition, had I been left in any doubt about the authority of the sources I had found, I could (and in my own professional area certainly would) have traced the sources back into the peer-reviewed journals where the original research had been reported. In that way I could have formed a judgement about the evidence base that supported the views I was being given.

The second important area where research skills can be seen at work in this example is in the ability to identify and refocus subsidiary questions as a result of research. A researcher has to be able to put herself in a position where she can see that, in spite of the fact that she has answered her original question, there are still issues that arise from the research so far. This process of using the information that has been collected and sorted to inform the next round of the research is typical of the research process. It is rarely possible to set out with a research question, and simply find the information that answers it.

It is in this process of interrogating the data, where the researcher, in effect, is in dialogue with the information that she is gathering, that the true spirit of the creative researcher is to be found. Certainly, Eve wanted to know about raised levels of blood antibodies, but once she had that information, what else would she want to know? Could there be some other concern, or counter-argument that would make this answer unsatisfactory?

This ability to see a sceptical rejoinder coming and to anticipate further questions as to whether a research answer is adequate is probably the most difficult skill to develop. My experience suggests that it gets no easier as time goes on. It is part of the human disposition to think that the case that one is arguing is obvious and not in much need of further amplification. It is similarly normal to take for granted much background information that one has come across in the course of one's research, which is not necessarily available to one's reader and critics. In those circumstances it is also perfectly natural that one's presentation of one's research results should be partial and flawed but that only one's audience will be able to spot those mistakes. Spotting shortcomings in one's own case is always the most difficult piece of research activity.

In the light of this example, every researcher would be well advised to take seriously the Red Queen's advice to Alice. When Alice is urged to believe something impossible, she, like so many researchers, argues that she is completely unable to believe something which is impossible. The Red Queen is horrified and suggests that it is only a matter of practice and that she herself believes six impossible things every day before breakfast. Every researcher should take a course in the Red Queen's exercise regime. Being able to believe impossible things, even if only for a short while, is a valuable tool in being able to sort, sift and evaluate information. How damaging would it be to find a website which produced evidence that undermined the case I am building? Why have I not found such a website? Had I better conduct a specific search for it (if only to reassure myself that there is no such website)?

There is a general misconception that research is designed to provide answers to questions. If one watches people in every variety of circumstance, one comes to the conclusion that they can generally find answers all too well. People do not like questions, and they are generally ready to close down any question with a definitive answer, however little they know about the subject. What marks out a good researcher is not the ability to answer questions; it is the ability to keep an open mind about a question until it has provided a basis for all the interesting enquiry that it can afford.

We talk now of 'lifelong education' as a process that can continue through life, rather than finish when one graduates from secondary school. One of the motivations for moving towards lifelong education rather than more traditional models, where you have all the education you need served up before you start work, is that nobody can prepare themselves for 50 or more years of work before they reach the age of 20. Changing patterns of career development also indicate that one will probably need to retrain for a major change of work two or three times.

Even if we restrict ourselves to the world of education, no training can prepare one for everything that will happen in a career. We prepare student teachers, in general, to deal with pupils with special educational needs, for example. But the range of special educational needs that a practising teacher will encounter is potentially huge, and any particular teacher will only encounter some of them, and at a rate and in an order that cannot be predicted. At periodic but unpredictable points in their subsequent careers, teachers will need updates on specific educational needs that they encounter.

The only way in which this makes sense is if we prepare teachers to be constant researchers, to collect and sift information about the issues that they encounter as they gather teaching experience.

If we now bring these ideas together, the kind of research skills that I described in the opening of this chapter are those that are needed by a professional for periodically refreshing her expertise. In such a system of reflective practitioners, who research their own practice and who monitor their own performance, quality assurance is distributed throughout the whole system. This self-regulation at an individual level can be integrated into a professional system that secures quality through aspiration to the highest standards of service, and the opportunities that it offers for self-fulfilment.

For most of the time, and all of the time in the present education system, we live with a completely different notion of quality assurance. We live with a system which is based on a notion of centralized control and accountability through lines of management responsibility. This is a system where targets are set, goals and outcomes specified, contracts set for 'deliverables', and professionals held to account for their performance against those targets. And, as I have commented before, those targets and goals are necessarily arbitrary because we do not have multicentred theories which are capable of handling rational grounds for setting targets.

Now, I think, we need to be very clear that targets and benchmarking are not necessarily bad in themselves. As I have noted in the context of Vygotsky's work on learning and teaching, there are some aspects of the process that are controllable and some that are not. Setting targets and instituting systems of accountability are appropriate for the parts of the educational process that are controllable, but are completely inappropriate for the parts of the process that are intrinsically uncontrollable. And, as I have noted, the point and purpose of education is the uncontrollable part of the process.

In the controllable 'interpersonal' cycle of learning, learning outcomes, targets and goals are not only acceptable but positively helpful. We have for too long run education so that those who can pick up the implicit messages, the hidden curriculum, are at an advantage. If we wish to take seriously the notion that access to education can be widened, then making as much as possible about the process explicit and public is the best way of improving the opportunities of those who do not have private access to an understanding of what the education process is 'really' about.

The problem is that the 'intrapersonal' cycle of learning cannot be controlled in this way, and attempting to control that part will not improve the learning: it simply stops it happening at all. And there is the additional difficulty that since education is a complex system and shows recursive symmetries, attempting to perfect systems of control at one level will have an impact upon all other levels in the system. Recursive symmetries are those patterns of similarities that are loosely connected and that one sees at different levels of magnification in complex systems (Turner 2004a: 169).

The result of the line of thought set out above is that it is a mistake to believe that error, untidiness, deviance or simply performance that we do not like can be controlled out of the system. We see this tendency to escalating control in many areas of society: increasingly stringent supervision of antisocial behaviour, anti-terror legislation, demands for ever-harsher punitive measures against criminals and growing use of CCTV. But in education this tendency is possibly seen at its strongest. Call parents of unruly pupils to account; remove teachers who are not performing to target; punish schools where there are pupils who cannot read out loud to the required standard; instigate a policy of zero tolerance and whole-school conformity.

But what we can see from viewing the education system as a complex system where the core activity of learning cannot be controlled is that these attempts to remove undesirable behaviour result in a removal of the activities that we most wish to promote. To put this another way, learning arises, according to Vygotsky, in a situation where there are multiple possible feedback loops, where one can reflect upon one's own motivation, substitute alternative conditioned responses and alter one's own behaviour at will. Systems with non-linear responses and multiple feedback loops are complex and tend towards behaviour that we describe as chaotic.

We know how to prevent chaotic behaviour, or at least to reduce its likelihood; we simply remove or reduce non-linear responses and multiple feedback loops. The more we can control those characteristics, the less likely is it that we see chaotic behaviour. So we certainly can control-out chaotic behaviour by reducing the complexity of the system, but we are almost certain to control-out learning at the same time, because the mechanisms that result in complex behaviour are the same mechanisms that result in learning. This is hardly surprising, as learning is a complex and chaotic process. Ironically, it may be the inefficiency and ineptitude of our teachers that has been the saving grace of our education system. Or rather, it may be the idiosyncrasy and eccentricity of great teachers that is important, not their 'competences'.

We have made the mistake of believing that misbehaviour and disorder are in some way 'errors' that can be removed from the system. This is perhaps a natural conclusion from a traditional view of science, that our goal is to understand and gain control of a clockwork world. It is possible that novelists have had a clearer vision of what success would mean, and have described what it would mean to teach in Stepford County High School or Midwych Primary. Rebellion and self-expression are an important, if risky, part of growing up and maturing, and can only be controlled at a high cost. And in this context I am not talking about a high cost in teachers' salaries or security systems; I am talking about the cost of preventing learning and maturation altogether.

In the past we have been able to manage this within a range of double standards. When young people on a council estate have gone binge-drinking and created a disturbance or broken some windows, this has clearly been blatant vandalism and the end of civilization as we know it. When the elite sportsmen of the rugby team have had a team celebration after a victory and broken some windows, this has clearly been an unfortunate result of some high-spirited young gentlemen letting off steam. We obviously do need to rethink this in an age when education has broadened to a mass system and more people may be affected by the behaviour of high-spirited young gentlemen and gentlewomen. But we cannot fool ourselves into believing that antisocial behaviour can be programmed out of society altogether. We need to be thinking about acceptable levels of misbehaviour, tolerable levels of risk and reasonable levels of interpersonal friction. And in research terms we need to be asking about the circumstances through which we can reduce unacceptable levels of each to acceptable levels.

The myth that total control of the system is achievable has taken hold, and is in danger of dominating how we run the education system, whether we consciously intend it or not. A good example of the unintentional application of the myth of total control is the rise of the use of league tables. Our higher education system was set up, as revised in 1992, to promote diversity of mission in the institutions of higher education that we have. Some institutions would prize research and the creation of new knowledge more than anything else, while others would promote social inclusion or public service. The advantage of having diversity of mission, and perhaps even a little lack of clarity about mission, is that it promotes complexity. Week by week, lecture by lecture, it is possible for a slightly different motivation to be called upon, a slightly different direction taken. At an institutional level, this might be compared with Vygotsky's notion that in gaining control of our own actions we learn how to substitute one conditioned response for another. The reflective researcher/practitioner who develops her own policies for action in dialogue with the data can be compared with the individual who learns how to focus their attention using learned, cultural symbols. Multiple feedback loops abound, and the system is chaotic.

And then those multiple and complex behaviours are used to construct a league table, either officially or unofficially, and a single criterion of success is derived from many. The different perspectives of the different participants are ignored. The values that are attached to different aspects of performance by different stakeholders are overruled. And discussion and debate about what the institution is trying to achieve is squeezed out of the system (Turner 2005). In short, league tables can become an instrument for the myth of total control, or even a mechanism whereby total control is re-established, even where that was not originally intended.

The myth that complex systems such as education can be totally controlled clearly does damage to those systems when it leads to policy that unintentionally prevents the core goals of the system being achieved. But the damage done by the myth of total control may be even more insidious than that. The idea that we can control systems that cannot be controlled is bound to lead to frustrated expectations and fruitless activity.

The idea that we can completely protect every child from the risk of encounters with strangers will lead us to remove children from learning opportunities, where they can learn how to handle difficult situations. But it may also lead to many adults growing up believing that their relationships can be controlled completely. While most of us come to realize that proper human relationships cannot be controlled without demeaning some of the parties to them, there appears to be a growing number of people who believe that their relationships can and should be kept totally under control. And what better way of making sure that my relationships are controllable, than to limit my relationships to young children and immature people who can be manipulated to my own ends? Far from reducing the risk to children and young people, the myth of total control may be increasing the number of inadequate people who cannot handle the complexity of real, fulfilling, human relationships, and seek instead to dominate young children. And that, in turn, may be increasing the risk to children from strangers, not reducing it.

If the myth of total control is growing in society in general, then it seems to be nowhere more apparent than in the education system. At the level of the national system, it may not be entirely clear what the intentions of policy-makers and politicians are. Measures to reduce central control, to create diversity of administrative measures, are frequently coupled with the introduction of national standards, goals and targets. The 1988 Education Reform Act lessened the control of local education authorities over school budgets at the same time as it introduced a national curriculum. And as has been noted, unofficial measures such as league tables may have a bigger effect than the formal policy measures introduced. But a majority of observers are of the opinion that central control has increased rather than decreased. There has been a rise in 'managerialism' in education, and it has displaced 'professional ethos' and 'collegiality'.

Perhaps more worrying is a tendency for education to recruit teachers who are attracted to the idea of total control; it may be a personality trait that is all too easily combined with an ambition to teach. What could be more attractive than the notion of shaping the next generation? Of being Svengali to not one but hundreds of protégées? And at one level that is part of the inevitable motivation of teachers. But it is surely counterproductive when a teacher comes to think of the successes of their pupils as their own. Teachers cannot control the reactions of their students, and should not be encouraged to believe that they can force young people to learn. Nor should they be told that it is acceptable to evaluate the quality of a teacher by the examination results achieved by their pupils. If a teacher's classes consistently achieve poorly, we should certainly ask what is going on, and whether there are ways of improving performance. Benchmarking is a perfectly sensible way of proceeding. But there are better ways of benchmarking that crude league tables (Turner 2005). And we should never lose sight of whose achievements an assessment actually records.

This line of argument brings me back to the question of quality assurance. If total control is impossible, what kind of quality assurance *is* possible? And the only conceivable answer is a system of quality assurance where the elements of reflection on action, and the motivation to improve all aspects of performance, is universally distributed. This is the only system of quality assurance that can function in a complex system.

This is not the same as arguing that all research should be at the classroom level. But it does mean that there needs to be the capacity to read and interpret research at the level of every classroom. This is not the same as saying that teachers need to be given 500-word summaries of research as a source of 'good practice'. Teachers need to be able to make judgements about what is best for their classrooms. And they need to be motivated to implement those ideas when they find them. This is the only kind of quality assurance that can work in the long-run.

Anecdotal evidence

One hardly needs anecdotal evidence of this tendency towards micromanaging every aspect of the educational system. It has even acquired its own name of the 'new managerialism'. In all aspects, increased paperwork, checklists and codes of practice proliferate. The will to control is part of our everyday experience of education. From the 180 or so competences that newly qualified teachers are supposed to exhibit, to the detailed specification of what people will have achieved by following a course of study, every aspect of education is becoming increasingly bureaucratized.

Now that is not to say that bureaucratization is all bad. Bureaucracy, in Weber's terms, is about removing personal privilege and providing clear, rule-governed systems that will treat people fairly in relation to their position, not in relation to their person or status. In this sense, specifying educational programmes in terms of learning outcomes so that what is on offer can be understood by those who come from families that have no experience of higher education may be a very good idea. Unfortunately, however, such systems can frequently become reduced to a simplified process of 'ticking boxes', a defensive management technique rather than an active way of increasing understanding of the system.

This is particularly true where systems produce a mass of information that illustrates the diversity of those systems. Schools produce data about performance of pupils in examinations and standardized tests, about indicators of social deprivation and of resource provision. This complex information needs to be actively interrogated, 'researched' in the sense that I have set out at the beginning of this chapter. But our impulse to control, and to place a market value on what we see, embraces the tendency to try to reduce this wealth of data to a single measure of performance. And having identified that measure of performance, to construct a league table.

A good university might be one that excels in research; that provides excellent teaching; that provides a supportive social environment for students from all backgrounds; that provides opportunities for all individuals to develop their skills in a very wide range of pursuits. But if we simply refer to a 'good university' or a 'world-class university' then there is normally very little doubt about which institutions we are referring to. We assume that all of those excellent qualities coexist in a handful of institutions, without very much evidence, on the grounds that those institutions have a high reputation and seem to appear regularly at the top of league tables that are published to make it easy for us to comprehend that complexity.

Promoting a quality system involves much more than simply measuring the performance of institutions on a wide range of dimensions. It means ensuring that professionals engaged in those systems have the research skills to interrogate that data, to form opinions and to debate reform procedures. In short, it means taking the concept of 'fitness for purpose' seriously. Attempting to measure the performance of a complex system should be the beginning of a debate about quality enhancement, not the end of it.

Prior research

There has been a good deal of research into league tables, including some that I have done myself. My own work in this area has been on the possibility of using data envelope analysis (DEA) for benchmarking purposes. DEA is a technique from operational research which is ideally suited for benchmarking in cases where there are no absolute standards of efficiency, and would therefore appear to be perfect for application to universities and schools.

Put very simply, DEA has a number of advantages over other methods for constructing benchmarks, in that it can accommodate both inputs and outputs, compares institutions with other similar institutions and embodies the multicentred dictum that there are many ways of being excellent.

On the negative side, although DEA is relatively easy to grasp in simple cases, for complex cases it can be very difficult to visualize what is happening, and it always requires quite sophisticated computer software. This is not a disadvantage in itself, and indeed sophisticated software is now becoming available at very reasonable prices, but it does mean that it may not always be easy to translate the results into terms that can be understood immediately and intuitively. However, such negative characteristics do not prevent researchers from using SPSS (Statistical Package for the Social Sciences), even if they cannot calculate a standard deviation, and rightly so.

The essential idea behind DEA is that different institutions might take a variety of inputs and convert them into a variety of outputs. For example, in the case of a university, the institution might take in a student body with certain prior examination results, and a staff body with certain qualifications and characteristics, and through an educational process produce outputs that can be evaluated such as a number of qualified graduates, research outputs that merit particular grades, teaching that is recognized to be of a high standard in teaching quality assessments, and so on. I have used for illustrative purposes a very simplified schema in which teaching quality divided by a measure of staff–student ratio is used as an indicator of how well universities turn resources into the output of teaching, while a measure of research quality divided by a measure of the staff–student ratio is used as an indicator of how well the institution turns resources into research outputs.

If we plot these two measures against each other for UK universities, a scatter-plot something like Figure 9.1 is produced.

Figure 9.1, simple though it is, illustrates the precise problem of using a league table based upon a single criterion for benchmarking purposes. The scatter-plot shows two fairly distinct 'clouds', one of research-focused institutions (towards the top of the figure), the other of teaching-led institutions (stretching out towards the right of the figure). Although these two types are fairly clearly discernible, the scatter-plot also illustrates the difficulties of producing an extremely simplified description of, say, three types of university – teaching-led, research-led and hybrid. In fact the boundaries of the different types are not clear and/or overlap.

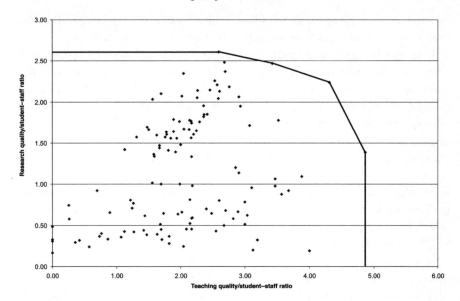

Figure 9.1   A scatter-plot of the relative performance of universities

The advantage of DEA is that it takes each institution that has an outstanding combination of the two measures to be counted as the most efficient, and a data envelope is drawn through those institutions (hence the name of the method). All other institutions are then compared with the part of the envelope that they are closest to, so that like is always compared with like. (This argument is set out in more detail in Turner 2005.)

In the present context, however, I only wish to stress two points. The first is that however DEA is interpreted, it never reduces performance to a single indicator, and the picture that one is left with is of institutions which might excel along a number of dimensions, or combinations of those dimensions. DEA, therefore, embodies the basic insight that there is more than one way in which an institution can be excellent; it is a multicentred method.

The other point that needs to be made is how the method can be used. Certainly, DEA can be used to evaluate how an institution compares with its peers, and hence to indicate measures that might be taken to secure improvement. But it should also be noted that there is considerable ambiguity, in an educational setting, as to what is an input and what is an output. It has been noted by others that the fact that an institution requires high entry qualifications may be seen as an input by some and an output by others. (Sarrico *et al.* 1997). For well-qualified students, and for their parents, high entry grades are an indicator of prestige, a promise of how a future graduate of the institution is likely to be viewed in the future, in fact an output. For the student who has struggled to secure good grades, they may be seen as an input, something that they bring to the process.

I am not the first to note that entry grades occupy this ambiguous position. But what struck me in the process of conducting the research on DEA was that every item appeared to have this double capability, of being viewed as either an input or an output. High staff–student ratio? That looks like lots of supportive staff from the perspective of the student, and therefore a result, or an output. But for the funding council or the senior management of the institution, it looks like a cost or an input. High level of investment in library resources? That must be an input from the point of view of the management team. But from the student's perspective it means that good management is making savings elsewhere in order to provide better front-line services, which is an output. And so on.

DEA not only allows us to process the idea that high quality can be achieved along a number of different dimensions, it also helps to frame the debate about what counts as high quality in an institution. Moreover, it makes clear that high quality is in the eye of the beholder, and that parents, students and teachers have different views of quality which need to be taken into account. Far from allowing us to reduce quality measures to a single performance indicator, or even a small number of performance indicators, multicentred approaches help us to frame resolutely multicentred descriptions of systems. Adopting them opens up discussion; it does not close discussion down.

Future directions for research

The future directions of this kind of research on benchmarking are fairly clear. I have demonstrated how DEA can be used as a multicentred approach to benchmarking and quality evaluation. That work has been rather crudely done through the reanalysis of data that had been collected for other purposes. Much better data is available through HESA (Higher Education Statistics Agency) than was available before, and it should be possible, relatively easily, to show how the method can be improved using better data.

Similarly, league tables having become such a ubiquitous method of measuring performance, DEA could be applied to many other fields of education.

At the same time, DEA can be used to examine how different groups of people conceive of quality in the institutions that they are connected to. A fully interactive benchmarking website that allowed the user to select which variables they thought to be important inputs and which important outputs, and even to select the range of comparator institutions on some criteria such as age or geographical location, could produce some very interesting perspectives on what people think is important in a high-quality school or university.

This might also lead into some interesting comparative work, to identify whether there is a range of inputs and outputs over which useful comparisons can be made on an international basis. Several rather crude national systems of comparison have been used, and it is clear that international comparisons are at least an aspiration of some newspapers, but whether there are convincing ways of conducting such international comparisons remains to be established.

It would not be proper to leave this topic without noting that DEA has been advanced before, but has also been met with some very robust criticisms. One could hardly, for example, imagine a more robust critique that that offered by Goldstein (1990). In a subsequent paper (Goldstein 1992: 43) he goes to the heart of the matter: 'The difficulty with DEA is that it cannot by itself establish the nature of the true relationship between the output and input variables.' But if participants cannot even agree which variables are input variables and which output variables, how can there be a 'true relationship' between inputs and outputs? DEA offers an opportunity, a framework within which, the politics of multiple perceptions of the education process can be examined. So long as we believe that there is one true relationship between the variables, one best way of increasing efficiency, then we will never be able to come to terms with the diversity that is implied in the term 'fit for purpose'.

So much effort and resource has been invested in single-centred approaches to educational research that there is a huge amount to be done, and very powerful interest groups committed to not doing it. We need extended programmes of research to even up this balance a little, so that the potential of multicentred research can be judged fairly and not simply dismissed.

But perhaps more importantly, multicentred research ought to focus upon how improvements can be achieved. There is a strong possibility that a management team that depended upon single-centred models of management would not be able to engage with a multicentred improvement plan, even if it was clearly an effective plan. It is for this reason that I have thought it necessary to try to integrate a vision of multicentred analysis that extended right across the educational system from individual learner to national policy. It also means that future research development will need to engage with all those facets.

Part 3

Theory into Practice

Chapter 10

Conclusions: Evidence-based Policy and Policy-based Research

Evidence-based policy

There has been an explosion of interest in 'evidence-based policy' (and evidence-based practice) with government agencies showing interest in how evidence can be used to ensure that interventions are effective. In the UK, the health service and prison service have shown particular interest, but education is not far behind. Government research funding has also been provided for research centres and study programmes in UK universities. Similar examples can be found in other parts of the world.

The implication of the phrase is fairly clear: that in choosing between policy alternatives, policy-makers at all levels should base their decisions in evidence which is supposed to be readily available to them. The interest in evidence-based policy, and the further implication that it is important because it has not been happening, draws two responses, depending upon the viewpoint of the observer. Policy-makers tend to argue that there is a dearth of research evidence, principally because researchers are too busy exploring esoteric topics or advancing their own careers to deign to produce anything approaching evidence that would be relevant in selecting policy. Researchers tend to bemoan the fact that policy-makers do not have any real interest in the evidence that research has produced, or at least they are only interested in evidence that supports the policy option that they have already selected.

What I want to suggest is that in this failure to match research evidence to policy researchers bear an important responsibility, perhaps the major responsibility. I want to suggest that this is not because they are researching the wrong things, or lacking an interest in practical results, but because they frame their theories in a way which is inappropriate. If researchers wish their research evidence to be used by policy-makers, they must first generate evidence in a way which is valuable to the policy-makers. In a word, they must undertake policy-based research.

The first thing to be noted here is that policy-makers may not know what evidence they need. They are as capable as researchers of falling into some of the fallacies and commonsense perspectives that bedevil researchers. If those policy-makers are also politicians, then they are more likely to fall into such traps. So producing policy-based research is not a question of producing what policy-makers want, much less of what they say they want.

In earlier chapters, I have suggested that the current research imagination is dominated by models that I have described as 'single-centred'. Single-centredness involves an assumption that if we could identify a homogeneous group of people, and we could expose them to similar influences and put them in a similar setting, we would expect them all to respond in identical ways. The corollary of this is that if we find a population that divides itself between two courses of action, it can be assumed that it was not a homogeneous population, and that one of the functions of research should be to identify the factor, either genetic or environmental, that separates the two groups. The use of the word 'factor' itself is indicative of the statistical heritage of such thinking in correlation studies and regression analysis. There is a commonsense model of research, based on such techniques, that sees the purpose of any investigation to see the identification of the causes of the outcomes that we observe.

Thus, to take one example from the popular sphere, if some people develop lung cancer and some do not, the purpose of research is to isolate and identify the factor or cause which allows us to differentiate between the two groups. The most obvious candidate for this cause is smoking. This would give us our first hypothesis, that smoking causes cancer. At the risk of overworking the point, smokers who developed cancer and non-smokers who did not would count as supporting evidence for the hypothesis, while non-smokers who developed cancer and smokers who did not would count as evidence to the contrary. And the policy which would follow from the hypothesis would be to discourage people from smoking.

However, as a single-centred solution to the problem that presented itself, this result is less than perfect; there is counter-evidence which includes non-smokers who develop lung cancer. We might then pursue a second refinement on our theory of identifying the factors or causes which distinguishes between those non-smokers who do develop cancer and those who do not. The most obvious candidate for this cause is smoking; not in this case active smoking or inhaling directly from cigarettes, but of passive smoking, the inhalation of second-hand smoke from other people. This gives us our second hypothesis that passive smoking causes cancer. And the evidence for this hypothesis is that there are non-smokers who develop lung cancer, together with the established fact of the first hypothesis, that inhaling tobacco smoke is, in general, harmful.

This leads to the rather curious conclusion that if we combine an established hypothesis with the evidence which contradicts it, we can produce a second, equally widely held hypothesis. I should perhaps make clear that I have no particular brief for the support of smoking. I am quite happy to believe that both active and passive smoking increase the likelihood of lung cancer. Nor do I object to any of the policies that are based on these hypotheses. I prefer to work in smoke-free environments, and have found anti-smoking campaigns positively helpful in my own efforts to give up smoking. My only complaint is that this very simple example shows what damage the logic of single-centredness does to our notions of an evidence base for policy. We have reached a point where we can accept, almost as a matter of common sense, two hypotheses which, together, rely upon the existence of a body of evidence which supports the one and contradicts the other.

It might be argued that I have overstated the case, and in particular that I have overstated the hypotheses. The hypotheses are not exactly as I have stated them, but should rather be understood as stochastic. Smoking increases the likelihood of developing cancer; all that is necessary for the support of this hypothesis is that a greater proportion of smokers should develop cancer.

I think that this line of argument has to be rejected. I think that we need to distinguish between the guiding principle or ideal of this kind of research, and the practical implementation. The guiding principle of such research depends upon the notion that hypotheses such as the ones that I have presented can be found. But researchers in this paradigm accept that, at the present time and with the present state of knowledge, there are limitations to the certainty that can be ascribed to such hypotheses. At present, not all the factors and causes have been identified, and this in turn is evidence of the complexity of medicine, education and the social sciences, when compared with something simple like physics or chemistry. (This argument is normally advanced by researchers who understand neither physics or chemistry.)

My argument is that the governing principle of single-centred research is that eventually all of the factors will be identified, and at that point it will be possible to differentiate exactly what the causes are that result in a person being in one group rather than another. And in arguing that case I would point to two very important pieces of evidence. The first is that any random variation which cannot be ascribed to an identified factor is described as 'error'. This is of course only a word, and it might not be wise to read too much into it, but it is indicative of an attitude that the stochastic nature of the hypotheses that we have is something that we anticipate eliminating in the future.

More important in this context is the second piece of evidence, the research effort that is thrown into finding those additional factors and causes. Dissatisfied with stochastic results, we insist upon finding further causes which will explain the differences between those who do and those who do not develop cancer: genetic endowment, diet, environmental exposure, and so on and so forth.

I think that Michael Bassey (2001) has correctly described this process as 'fuzzy probability'. In our efforts to allocate people to the correct group (going to develop cancer and not prove) we use the tools that we have (our first hypothesis) and can correctly allocate, perhaps, 80 per cent of people to the correct group. If we add more information (our second hypothesis) we might be successful in allocating 90 per cent to the correct group. By adding another hypothesis about genetic propensity we might manage to be correct in 95 per cent of cases. The fuzziness at the edge of our research means that we cannot expect to be perfectly correct all the time. But with time and diligence we can expect to reduce the fuzziness. And I stress again that at the heart of the method, once the fuzziness has been stripped away, or hiding somewhere near the centre of present fuzziness, is the precise, single-centred answer. There is a constellation of causes of cancer that will one day be identified.

I have chosen an example from medicine rather than from education because it is clear and widely accepted. I could, with one or two minor differences, have selected corresponding hypotheses from education. 'Progressive' teachers stimulate their pupils to better results, 'whole-class' teaching leads to improvement in reading scores, children from homes where there are more books are more successful at school, boys have fewer examination successes than girls, or any one of a number of similar hypotheses that relate to the causes of educational outcomes could be examined. The most important difference, however, between the educational case and the medical case is that the hypotheses are very much fuzzier, the errors are very much bigger and the work that is still to be done is greater. In national studies, isolating the factors that account for even 50 per cent of the variation in student performance would be a triumph; in international studies explaining 20 per cent of the variation would be a miracle. In education in general we are saved the difficulty of evaluating the quality of the evidence, because the evidence can only explain a tiny fraction of what we observe as outcomes. Because the majority of what we see in schools can only be described as 'error' or 'fuzziness', we rarely need to confront the single-centredness which is the guiding principle of educational research.

In summary, this discussion of the debate around smoking and cancer highlights the role of single-centredness in the research models that are being applied at the moment. The idea that the outcomes for homogeneous groups should be homogeneous, and the corollary that a group for which the outcomes are heterogeneous cannot itself be homogeneous, dominates our thinking about research. This is true at the level of design and overall direction, even if it is accepted that for practical reasons we are a long way away from removing all the fuzziness. And in the process of pursuing that search for unambiguous causes, a good deal of damage is done to the logic of evidence-based research. Evidence is either ignored or used very selectively, as it has to be to sustain single-centred approaches. The long-term damage that this does is primarily to our sense of how evidence can and should be used in developing policy.

Single-centred research

Although this situation may appear to be a poor starting point for evidence-based educational policy, the true effect of single-centred approaches is, in fact, very much worse. Even where it is generally accepted that the available evidence supports a hypothesis, the move from hypothesis to policy is not straightforward.

In the first place, the hypothetical causes of educational disadvantage may not be amenable to policy intervention. This is most obviously the case where poor performance in school is associated with a variable such as gender or race. If girls and boys are different populations with regard to school performance, and the mean performance of girls on examinations is better, then what is to be done? The most obvious response is to suggest an intervention to support the disadvantaged group, and this would be in line with our emotional and moral reaction to such a situation. However, it is worth thinking about the evidence base for such a response. If the hypothesis linking gender and school performance is a real one (as opposed to a spurious proxy for some other relationships) then it cannot be changed by an intervention. And if an intervention is effective, then it implies that the original hypothesis was flawed, or poorly specified. And the main damage, as usual, is done to our sense that policy can be based on evidence. In this case the effectiveness of the proposed policy depends upon the fallibility of the hypothesis that the evidence is supposed to be supporting.

In practice, the response to such a situation, where the variable involved is not amenable to manipulation through policy, is to bring the cause under some general heading, such as sexism or racism, which is yet more poorly specified and even less amenable to policy intervention. However, once such an umbrella cause has been identified it will normally be possible to introduce almost any policy that one could wish, irrespective of any evidential base. In this way fashionable orthodoxies can be produced, whether they are 'whole-school' policies on bullying or increased accountability, without worrying too much about whether the evidence actually supports them.

The situation is hardly any better where the hypothetical factors identified in educational research are capable of manipulation through policy. A fairly well-established hypothesis is that children who come from homes where there are at least ten books are more likely to be successful in education. To my knowledge, no educational programme has ever been introduced to distribute free books to households that had fewer than ten books in order to improve educational performance. The policy, although based on evidence, would be widely regarded as foolish for a number of reasons: the policy has no intuitive link with performance in schools, the presence of books in a household is a proxy measure for something else (educational level of parents or value placed on reading), or it would divert precious resources from other areas where, it is supposed, they would be more effective.

In other words, we all know at some level that an attempt to base policy upon evidence, using single-centred models, is flawed, and needs to be controlled by some broader evaluative faculty. But we maintain single-centredness as the dominant style and rationale for educational research. At a theoretical level, the first casualty is our ability to develop evidence-based policy in a rational and effective way. But this is by no means the most important casualty in terms of policy. Our ambivalence to educational research in general is extremely marked, with most people picking out for commendation research that supports their prejudices. Politicians are particularly prone to this, and to being at a loss to understand why, if they have policies that are so good, the population at large cannot understand how wonderful they really are.

The idea that, in the final analysis, everything must have a cause, or explanatory factors, promotes the 'blame culture' that has been so much criticized of late. Nothing is any longer viewed as an accident, or a coincidence. If a supposedly homogeneous population does not behave homogeneously on one dimension, then there must be an underlying cause at work, and the search for that cause is a legitimate subject for research, or, in the absence of research, speculation.

The dependence upon single-centred approaches to research, and by extension to all forms of understanding, can also be seen to promote an 'all-or-nothing' response to policy questions. If it is economically advantageous for one resident of Athens to move to London to seek work, then it is supposed that it will be advantageous for every Athenian to move to London. On the basis of such reasoning, it is relatively easy to raise concern that London will be flooded with itinerant Greeks. At some level we know that this is nonsense, and that the mass migration of people must eventually have such an impact upon employment opportunities in both Athens and London that the incentive to migrate no longer operates. But the logic of the single-centred argument is inescapable: there is a homogeneous population of Greeks who have equally strong desires to secure their financial futures; some Greeks (or at least one Greek – you may know one or have read about one in the newspaper) have migrated to London to seek work; and, therefore, there are millions more for whom migration would be the logical next step.

In the educational field such reasoning is also rife. There is a homogeneous group of working-class children seeking university places; of those working-class children who currently attend university, those who attend ancient universities reap the highest return on their investment; therefore working-class children should apply for places in ancient universities or none. Or, there is a homogeneous population of schools; some have chosen to opt out of local authority control (or have applied to become beacon schools or have attracted private investment); therefore all the other schools will follow (or should follow, or are wilfully resisting following for partisan political reasons and it has to stop).

Overall such approaches to the link between research evidence and policy are not at all helpful. What I am arguing here is that the structure of single-centred models of research means that they provide 'evidence' which is almost universally irrelevant to policy-makers. A first step in this direction would be to adopt frameworks for research which are more likely to produce evidence on which policy can be based. And what I am advocating is the opposite of single-centredness, which for obvious reasons I call multicentredness.

Multicentred research

At the core of a multicentred approach is an intuition or imagination that a group of people might be homogeneous, and might find themselves in an identical situation, and yet might choose (and therefore have) different outcomes. Identical twins might have identical genetic inheritance, be exposed to identical environmental influences, and yet in spite of that (perhaps even because of that) have very different personalities. As the youngest of four brothers I had the opportunity to observe many aspects of educational development. As far as I can tell there was little to choose between us in terms of native intelligence or talent, and yet we were, in descending order of age, a chemist, a geographer, an artist and musician, and a physicist. I often wonder whether those different outcomes were not prompted by our very similarities, that each one in turn chose a field of endeavour where he could escape from comparisons with older brothers. That nagging question, as to whether what others in your group do can influence your own outcomes, is at the heart of a multicentred approach.

Most of the interesting policy questions that we face in education are multicentred questions. What proportion of applicants from working-class backgrounds should we expect to apply to study in ancient universities? How would that compare with those from middle-class backgrounds? Do we have any way of understanding why the proportion of school leavers who decide to enter the labour-market directly at 16 is as it is? Do we have in our hands the levers of policy that would enable us to change those proportions in any of these cases?

In a practical sense, we almost always have policy levers in our hands, and they are normally financial. If we increase the cost of a course of action, or reduce the financial benefits from it, then we expect the number of people taking that course of action to decrease (except, of course, when we do not, and we hold firmly to the belief that the reason qualified teachers will not teach has nothing to do with the poor pay of teachers, and the reason more people do not attend university has nothing to do with charging fees). But in theoretical terms, we simply have no way at all of dealing with the proportions of people making a choice. We have no theories that will explain why 10 per cent of people choose this course of action, or what we should do to change that 10 per cent into 20. And this is particularly curious when we have governments that are obsessed by the idea of setting targets; the one thing that we can be sure of is that when a government sets a target, such as 50 per cent of an age cohort in university, that target has been plucked out of the air with absolutely no foundation in theory or evidence whatsoever.

It is, perhaps, particularly worth noting that a multicentred approach is of most value in policy terms when the issues under consideration are not amenable to policy control within a single-centred framework of analysis. For example, the point has already been made that where race or ethnicity is an element of the analysis it is not at all clear what can be done in policy terms.

Afro-Caribbean boys are three or four times more likely to be excluded from secondary schools as their white peers. In anybody's book, this would be prima-facie evidence that there is racial discrimination of some kind here. But from a policy point of view it makes a very great difference, or at least should make a very great difference, whether we are looking at present racial prejudice in the school or anticipated future racial discrimination in the labour market. If Afro-Caribbean boys are going to face discrimination in the labour market, if they are not going to be adequately rewarded for the educational qualifications they achieve, if they are going to find their fellow students promoted over them even though they have poorer qualifications, what percentage of those Afro-Caribbean males would we expect to drop out of school, react aggressively to the suggestion that they need education, and adjust their value-system to exclude educational qualifications? Of course, these are hypothetical questions, but if we did have a good knowledge of what happens in the labour market, we still would not be able to anticipate what backwash effect that might have on the school system. And without that crucial piece of information, we have no way of knowing whether the schools are explicitly racist, or whether the schools are equal opportunity institutions, and different groups use them differently to prepare themselves unequally for a segmented labour market. And no amount of press coverage, or media interviews with ministers about racism in the schools, or any number of statements from heads and governors of schools can possibly address that question. What is needed is good policy-linked research that can tell us what proportion of a particular school-age population could be expected to reject education in the light of which anticipated labour-market rewards. That is, what is needed is multicentred research.

Policy-based research

What I have offered is a critique of the vast majority of educational research, on the grounds that it is single-centred. In passing, I have set out a research agenda for multicentred research. And what is most needed is a new and fundamental way of imagining educational policy issues. We need to be able to envisage that a homogeneous group could be exposed to the same influences and environmental settings, and yet should part company and go different ways.

In previous writing I have suggested that we naturally think in multicentred ways in some other areas of life (Turner 2004b). When we consider the flow of traffic through a network of roads, nothing would strike us as odder than that all the cars should be on one road and none on the others.

Traffic naturally distributes itself between the available routes, until there is no advantage to a driver to move from one route to another. New road-works will encourage some motorists to move away from their usual route and try a different one. Other drivers will leave home early or late to avoid the congestion. And we would not think of conducting personality tests on drivers to determine which kind of person favours driving down the main road and which type prefers the back roads. (Well, as educationists we might, but traffic engineers would not waste their time on it.) But we think nothing of asking what it is that has made a newly qualified teacher turn off the main highway rather than follow it into a career in school teaching.

So we need to take on board that a homogeneous group may divide itself between possible outcomes, and there be no criterion on which we can separate the groups or at least no criterion that will rise, or perhaps could possibly rise, above our theoretical radar and be detected. But for policy purposes, there is no need to know why one group goes one way rather than the other, any more than there is a need to understand the preferences of drivers before designing a bypass. What is important is how the homo-geneous group divides itself between the options; what proportion goes into teaching, and what proportion does not.

Multicentred research can address that important policy-oriented ques-tion, and single-centred research cannot. If we expect policy-makers to use research evidence to develop evidence-based policy, then we need to provide them with evidence that is capable of acting as the basis for policy. We need policy-based research. By which of course I mean that we need multicentred research. We cannot expect our politicians and policy-makers to make bricks without straw, or evidence-based policy without policy supporting research.

It should perhaps be stressed that policy-making is policy-making and research is research, and the two processes can never be integrated into a single, seamless, decision-free robe. Even if we knew how to adjust employ-ment incentives to move 90 per cent of newly qualified teachers into a career in schools, instead of 80 per cent, that would not mean that we should do so, or even that we could afford to do so. The purpose of policy-based research is to show policy-makers which policy levers they might reason-ably be expected to operate, and with what anticipated effect. Policy deci-sions will remain political and can never be reduced to a technical-rational calculation.

But it also needs to be borne in mind that this is not a unique feature of multicentred research. Single-centred research can be equally difficult, and perhaps even more dangerous in terms of policy direction. Suppose that a university, under considerable pressure to reduce its drop-out rate, was to conduct research into what separated those who left programmes from those who stayed. And suppose, furthermore, that the research showed that a variable that was not capable of policy manipulation could account for much of the difference: for instance, that females were more likely to abandon their studies than males. It is a short step from there to adopting an admissions policy which solves the drop-out rate issue by admitting only male students. The dangers of jumping from a research result to a policy are ubiquitous, and exist in single-centred research as much as in multi-centred research.

In this chapter I have set out the rationale for developing new multicentred research models to provide a theoretical underpinning for education policy. I have chosen some illustrative examples to indicate why this is necessary, and how it might be effective as a strategy. In the preceding chapters I have examined a range of educational settings to show how multicentred research could throw new light on familiar situations and how it might support the formulation of imaginative policies for improving education.

But imagining multicentred research is only a small part of the task. Doing it is much more. It has been my intention to show how a research question could be conceptualized, the implications for collecting data, and the way in which the possible outcomes might be used to inform policy. What we will actually find if and when we start conducting multicentred educational research is a matter that can only be anticipated imperfectly, and is obviously crucial to further developments. Very little multicentred research has been done, almost none of it in the area of education policy. Moving to multicentred models would involve looking at issues in different ways: ways that have passed single-centred researchers by as they have collected data which has been suitable for their imagining of the issues, but cannot normally be recast for those new ways of imagining.

For this reason, this book is not and cannot be a book of answers. It can and does suggest novel ways of looking at old problems. It can and does challenge many preconceptions about how education policy is viewed. But it also raises many questions that cannot be answered, and that in the answering of which yet more questions will be brought to light. This cannot be a quick and simple process. Single-centred research has been at the centre of the policy-maker's mental toolkit since at least the time of Aristotle. We cannot expect multicentred research to leap fully-formed to answer the questions that single-centred research has so far failed to answer.

In this book I have addressed a range of policy issues at different levels – classroom, school, whole system and individual learning – and the possible linkages between levels. I have provided some anecdotal evidence and reviewed some previous research that suggests that multicentred research could offer a way of developing a fuller understanding of how these policy issues interact. I confess that this has been an extremely ambitious canvas upon which to paint a research agenda. Only two circumstances can really justify tackling such a complex collection of issues.

The first circumstance is that teachers are expected to manage all of these issues already. If there is a social ill, from supposed lowering standards of manners to preparing for technological change, teachers are expected to provide the answer. And if the problem persists, of course, teachers are to blame.

And not only are teachers supposed to have access to all this specialized understanding, everybody else thinks that they have it too, as a result of having at one time or another attended a school. Politicians, parents, pundits and political advisers all think that they could manage education better, if only the teachers could be controlled and prevented from introducing their own, cranky ideas into the process. 'Teacher-proofing' the educational system has been a major thrust of national policy in many countries over the last 50 years.

Against that ambition, or assumption, of knowledge of how the education system works, and how policy should steer it, we have to admit that the actual, positive results of policy research have been minimal. In spite of decades of single-centred research, our understanding of policy issues and of how to manage educational settings could not be described as good. Multi-centred research offers the possibility of developing the expert knowledge that teachers really need to improve the educational system. Revell (2005) has suggested that teachers need to develop a clear body of professional knowledge and professional structures, so that they, as a profession, can avoid being at the whim of every passing political fashion. If professional teachers had an understanding of their own sphere of activity, in the same way as doctors or lawyers do, the continuity and performance of the educational system could be substantially improved. This amounts to a redefinition of the role of the professional teacher. I stress the word 'professional' here, because Revell does, too. He suggests that we need to identify what a teacher really does, or should do, and that involves making clear the distinction between a professional teacher, who plans, regulates and manages learning situations, and instructors, who simply teach in an institutional framework designed by the professionals. Unfortunately, while Revell argues the case that such professionalism is essential to the improvement of education, he is not so strong on what the content of that professional activity should be. Multicentred research provides at least the possibility that the gap that Revell has identified could be filled.

The other circumstance that justifies trying to tackle such a broad range of topics is that these are in important ways very strongly connected. At the heart of education is the process of learning how to control and manage ourselves, as described through the theories of Vygotsky. But this is not only a process of learning to manage oneself, but of learning how to project oneself, and in that process of learning to be oneself. And how those engaged in education view themselves is central to a range of important issues, including whether a student decides to pay attention to this lesson or to that, whether a teacher decides to stress this part of the curriculum or that, whether a teacher decides to dedicate themselves to the advancement of education in the inner city or cultivate a love of learning in a suburban private school. And achieving not simply a mass system of education but a high-quality mass system of education depends upon the teachers achieving the ultimate level of self-management, the ability to function as a self-regulating professional. As in a holographic image, the whole of the education system is reflected, and can be observed, in each part.

This conclusion, and the contents of this book in general, may still be too theoretical for the tastes of many readers. A title such as *Theory and Practice of Education* may have promised, to some readers, something much more firmly rooted in classroom practice, and 'how to do it'. Although much of what I have written is built upon practical concerns and issues that face teachers and policy-makers in their everyday business, I would not claim to have offered direct prescriptions for such practice.

On the other hand, I would claim that what I have set out in this book should have a very profound impact on practice, and on the way that we conduct the educational endeavour. Looking at education through the lens of multicentred theory should change everything. It should change the way that we frame research questions, and it should change the way we seek to conduct educational research in order to inform policy. But above all, it should move us away from the sense that difference is always pathological. It should enable us to see the value in diversity and difference.

But the biggest change in practice would be brought about if policy-makers recognized that complex systems, whether they are individual people or whole educational systems, cannot be improved by ever stricter management regimes. Curricula cannot be teacher-proofed, accountability cannot be tightened indefinitely, and sometimes accidents just happen.

References

Bassey, M. (2001) 'A solution to the problem of generalisation in educational research: fuzzy prediction', in *Oxford Review of Education*, 27.1: 5–22.

Cavanagh, M. (2002) *Against Equality of Opportunity* (Oxford: Oxford University Press).

Derrida, J. (1978) *Writing and Difference* (London: Routledge & Kegan Paul).

DfES (2006) *Further Education: Raising Skills, Improving Life Chances* (Norwich: HMSO) and also available at www.dfes.gov.uk/publications/furthereducation/ (accessed 20 September 2006).

Dweck, C. S. (2000) *Self-Theories: Their Role in Motivation, Personality and Development* (Hove: Taylor & Francis).

Einstein, A. (1920) *Relativity: The Special and General Theory – A Popular Exposition by Albert Einstein* (London: Methuen).

Fontana, D. (1994) *Managing Classroom Behaviour* (Leicester: BPS Books).

Gambetta, D. (1987) *Were They Pushed or Did They Jump?* (Cambridge: Cambridge University Press).

Goldstein, H. (1990) 'DEA: a response', in *Evaluation and Research in Education*, 6.1: 43–4.

—— (1992) 'Data envelopment analysis: an exposition and a critique', in *Evaluation and Research in Education*, 4.1: 17–20.

Gorard, S. (2006) 'Value-added is of little value', *Journal of Educational Policy*, 21.2: 233–41.

Halliday, J. (2005) 'The Nature of Educational Theory and Practice', in *Learning for Democracy*, 1.1: 117–24.

Honan, E. (2006) 'Teachers as bricoleurs resisting mandated curriculum', in J. Satterthwaite *et al.* 2006.

House of Commons Select Committee on Education and Skills (2006) Minutes of Evidence, Examination of Witnesses Questions 327–39, available at www.publications.parliament.uk/pa/cm200506/cmselect/cmeduski/478/6011811.htm (accessed 20 September 2006).

Killeen, J. (1996) 'Career theory', in A. G. Watts, Bill Law, J. Killeen, J. M. Kidd and R. Hawthorn (1996) *Rethinking Careers Education and Guidance: Theory, Policy and Practice* (London: Routledge), pp. 46–71.

Law, B. (1996) 'A career-learning theory', in A. G. Watts, Bill Law, J. Killeen, J. M. Kidd and R. Hawthorn (1996) *Rethinking Careers Education and Guidance: Theory, Policy and Practice* (London: Routledge), pp. 46–71.

Mead, G. H. (1967) *Mind, Self and Society* (London and Chicago, IL: University of Chicago Press).

Mueller, C. M. and Dweck, C. S. (1997) unpublished data, cited in Dweck 2000.

Osborne, A. (1976) *8080 Programming for Logic Design* (Berkeley, CA: Osborne).

Revell, P. (2005) *The Professionals: Better Teachers, Better Schools* (Stoke-on-Trent: Trentham Books).

Richmond, C. (2002) 'The balance model: minimalism in behaviour management', in Rogers, B. *Teacher Leadership and Behaviour Management* (London: Paul Chapman Publishing), pp. 53–70.

Rieber, R. W. (ed.) (1997) *The Collected Works of L.S. Vygotsky, Volume 4: The History of the Development of Higher Mental Functions*, trans. M. J. Hall (New York: Plenum Press).

Rogers, B. (2002) *Teacher Leadership and Behaviour Management* (London: Paul Chapman).

Sarrico, C. S., Hogan, S. M., Dyson, R. G. and Athanassopoulos, A. D. (1997) 'Data envelope analysis and university selection', *Journal of the Operational Research Society*, 48: 1163–77.

Satterthwaite, J. Martin, W. and Roberts, L. (eds) (2006) *Discourse, Resistance and Identity Formation* (Stoke-on-Trent: Trentham Books).

Turner, D. A. (1988) 'A game theory model of student decisions to leave school at 16 plus', in *Educational Research*, 30.1: 65–71.

—— (1990) 'Game theory in comparative education: prospects and propositions', in J. Schriewer (ed.), *Theories and Methods in Comparative Education*, 2nd edn (Frankfurt/ New York: Peter Lang), pp. 143–63.

—— (2004a) *Theory of Education* (London: Continuum).

—— (2004b) 'Alternative structures for lifelong learning', in *New Era in Education*, 85.1 (April): 14–15.

—— (2005) 'Benchmarking in universities: league tables revisited', in *Oxford Review of Education*, 31.3: 353–71.

Wainwright, H. and Elliott, D. (1982) *The Lucas Plan: A New Trade Unionism in the Making?* (London: Allison & Busby).

Wolfgang, C. H. (2001) *Solving Discipline and Classroom Management Problems: Methods and Models for Today's Teachers* (New York: John Wiley).

Index